LOVE, CELIBACY
and the
INNER MARRIAGE

Marie-Louise von Franz, Honorary Patron

**Studies in Jungian Psychology
by Jungian Analysts**

Daryl Sharp, General Editor

LOVE, CELIBACY
and the
INNER MARRIAGE

John P. Dourley

A portion of the research for this work was done at the Graduate
Theological Union in Berkeley and at the C.G. Jung Institute in San
Francisco, on a grant from the Social Sciences and Humanities
Research Council of Canada.
    Some of the material that appears here was originally presented
in public lectures.

Canadian Cataloguing in Publication Data

Dourley, John P.
    Love, celibacy and the inner marriage

(Studies in Jungian psychology by Jungian analysts; 29)

Includes bibliographical references and index.

ISBN 0-919123-28-7

1. Jung, C. G. (Carl Gustav), 1875–1961.
2. Psychology and religion.   3. Love—Religious
aspects.   4. Mechthild, of Magdeburg, ca. 1212–ca.
1282.   I. Title.   II. Series.

BF51.D68 1987   150.19′54   C87-094478-9

INNER CITY BOOKS
Box 1271, Station Q, Toronto, Canada M4T 2P4
Telephone (416) 927-0355

Honorary Patron: Marie-Louise von Franz.
Publisher and General Editor: Daryl Sharp.
Business Development: Vicki Cowan.
Editorial Board: Fraser Boa, Daryl Sharp, Marion Woodman.
Production Assistants: David Sharp, Ben Sharp.

INNER CITY BOOKS was founded in 1980 to promote the understanding and
practical application of the work of C.G. Jung.

Cover: Alchemical representation of the *anima mundi* (world soul).
Woodcut in Thurneisser zum Thurn, *Quinta essentia* (1574).

Index by Daryl Sharp

Printed and bound in Canada by Webcom Limited

Contents

See final pages for descriptions of other Inner City Books

Jung at the age of 75

1

Jung and the Coincidence of Opposites:
God, Universe and Individual

In the common thought of today, God, universe and individual are usually considered, where they are considered at all, as opposites, as discontinuous—neither sharing a common ground nor taking part in any common being. The brunt of Western theology, and the cultural consciousness to which it has contributed, conceive of God as so transcending the universe and the individual that the latter two come to be seen as contingent products of an arbitrary divine creativity, an afterthought to Trinitarian self-sufficiency.

In severing the immediate and ontological link between the divine and the human, this kind of theological imagination has divorced the individual from a sense of his or her immediate continuity both with the divine and with the universe. The individual is cut adrift in an atomistic, unrelated cosmos emptied of any unifying or communion-making divine ground. The consequence is one of alienation in which the individual, dubiously gifted with self-consciousness, looks out, from a self-enclosed and lonely isolation, upon the immensities of an alien universe, peopled by equally isolated fellow human beings and, somewhere, by a God who presides from beyond over a multiplicity which proceeds from his hands but is divested of his being.

In this view individual, universe and God remain strangers in principle, and the approach of any of the three to the others needs be an experience of invasion, intrusion, manipulation or, in the case of God, omnipotent coercion.

In this chapter I will present a synopsis of the model of the psyche as conceived by Carl Jung, and suggest that the most distinguishing feature of his thought is the teleology or direction he discerns in the movement of the psyche to its maturation. In response to the perhaps too bleak description of modern consciousness I have drawn in my opening paragraph, I will concentrate on those features

7

of Jung's thought which contend that the maturational *telos* of the human psyche is toward a state of consciousness in which the individual draws progressively nearer to an inner source, at once the source of all consciousness and so of whatever meaning exists in the universe.

In this process the individual comes to a more residual experience of that point at which one's personal being intersects with the divine, and through it with all that is and can be in the human and natural world. This process of self-discovery entails the discovery of one's native divinity, experienced as a greater appropriation of one's personal wholeness. This experience inevitably carries with it an intensified compassion for the totality beyond one's person, because through it the individual approaches within the source of the all beyond. In addition, such an experience can heal the wounds inflicted on our collective Western consciousness by our mainstream theological imagination, which sees God, universe and individual as totally separable and so authors that alienation which must result when centers of consciousness face each other as "wholly other."

For Jung this state of consciousness is approached at the end of a long and arduous work upon oneself. It is a work that centers on the dialogue between the ego and that autonomous power which, in his view, transcends the ego and gives both birth and rebirth to it, that is, the power of the unconscious. Sometimes the dialogue is undertaken voluntarily. Sometimes it is forced upon the ego when it lives too far from, or actually opposes, the wholeness of the personality proferred to it by the Self. But wherever the dialogue is begun and followed through, it works to center the individual by relating him or her to all the reaches of a fuller personal realization and, in so doing, relates the centered individual to the full reaches of humanity itself.

I will briefly describe the major powers encountered in this inner dialogue and chart the direction in which the dialogue with them might move. I will then illustrate this movement with examples of dreams drawn from one of Jung's most famous cases. The movement of the dream sequence in this case culminates in one of the most striking images of the Self to be found in Jung's work. And so I will comment on the implications of this image and of related images of the Self in the light of how they tend to picture the relationship of God, individual and universe. I will then draw some tentative conclusions in the areas of philosophy, religious speculation and psychology from these sides of Jung's thought.

Let us begin then with a description of the Jungian conception of the unconscious and of the powers that enliven it. Among the various reasons Jung gave for his break with Freud was his growing sense that the unconscious contained a stratum or layer deeper than Freud's model of the subconscious could encompass.[1] Jung was to call this the collective unconscious. In this level of the psyche Jung located the archetypes and strove through many images and formulations to describe what they were. At times he describes them as the structures of the unconscious which are the *facultas preformandi*, the faculty of preforming, from which the repetitive yet varying symbols of belief and patterns of behavior proceed into consciousness.[2] Jung also describes the archetypes as psychoid.[3] By this he means they are unknowable in themselves but knowable through the similarities and likenesses in their products, namely, the symbols, myths, rites, folklore, religions and dreams they produce, or are capable of producing, in all times and cultures.[4]

As Jung conceives them, the archetypes are invested with great energy and when activated are responsible for man's sense of the numinous, which Jung equated with human religious experience in whatever form it occurs.[5] This numinous power is of sufficient force to convince anyone touched by it that he or she has been visited by the gods. Since this experience proceeds from the same archetypes which nightly produce the symbolic figures who make up our dream dramas, Jung was of the opinion that in our sleep we are addressed by the same gods who have revealed themselves to mankind in all the forms of its historical religions. Both dream and revelation proceed from the same source—the collective unconscious—working in the depth of each individual to lead that individual into the discovery and enactment of his or her personal myth and eternal truth.

If we follow Jung into the depths of the unconscious on the journey he took in the years following the break with Freud, what do we find? What Jung met personally is recorded in the chapter entitled "Confrontation with the Unconscious" in his autobiographical *Memories, Dreams, Reflections.*[6] The scene there is messy with the spontaneity and life the unconscious always shows in its immediate manifestations. But based on his personal and sustained experience of its powers, Jung went on to draw a map of the geography of the unconscious and to identify many of its inhabitants. This pioneer work has proven to be of assistance to those who have come after him in their own personal journeys, and to those who lead others in theirs.

If we approach the unconscious schematically the first power that may rise to greet us is the shadow. In dreams it is personified by someone of the same gender as the dreamer. It usually represents some aspect of the personality needing development and admission into consciousness, or some aspect of the dreamer's ego that is already apparent but working to the person's detriment. In Jung's understanding of the shadow one can see his basic understanding of the relation between the ego and the unconscious. The latter always works to compensate the former by leading it toward wholeness, equilibrium and relatedness, but it often begins this work through the revelation of one's shadow to oneself, and this is rarely complimentary to one's conscious self-evaluation—to one's cherished ideals or self-esteem. Confrontation with one's shadow is so frequently abrasive because it often takes the form of an attack by the unconscious on an ego clinging to the self-truncation needed for initial development, but now no longer adequate to the demands of the emerging Self.

Thus a man who dreams of a brute attacking his wife might look into his own attitude toward the feminine. A woman who dreams of a miser aunt who died of a heart attack might look into her own generosity and the state of her heart, at a level deeper than its physical condition. More positively, someone who dreams of an admired friend whose capacities always seem beyond the reach of the dreamer might reconsider and wonder if anything the friend can do the dreamer can't do better or at least as well. And, a much more common phenomenon, one who dreams frequently of his or her worst enemy, or most repulsive acquaintance, might look long and hard to see how the hated and repellent other might well be a missing link in the process of taking possession of one's own wholeness. For, if we do not make friends with the enemy, as the New Testament advises, then the enemy will surely turn us over to the judge and to the torturer.

If the shadow is not embraced as one's potential—both good and bad—then it is encountered as destroyer—destroyer of the one-sidedness on which a life is built. Paradoxically, this is the very one-sidedness which may be necessary to win one's place in the sun in the first half of life, but in which one is too frequently imprisoned in the second half. Too often, our early foundation becomes our later coffin.

Continuing our schematic trip into the underworld, the next major figure encountered is that of the inner contrasexual—the woman who dwells in the masculine psyche, the man who dwells in the feminine psyche. A conscious relationship with this figure has the quality of an inner marriage. In the making of this inner marriage Jung locates, in my opinion, the most important movement of the psyche. Where the ego can enter into an abiding relationship with the inner man or woman, the unconscious shows its most positive face. It supports the ego, enlivens it, yields up its wealth and riches. But where this mystical marriage, the *mysterium coniunctionis,* fails, the ego loses, sooner or later, its energy, its taste for life, its ability to go on.

Life lived at the ego level, away from the inner love affair, may continue for some time and even appear successful. For instance a one-sided intellectualism can yield rich rewards in an intellectual atmosphere precisely because it is one-sided. And, if to be human were to be only intellectual, it might prove ultimately satisfying. But since to be fully human means more than living at the level of any single one, or even all, of the developed sides of the ego, the failure to make the connection with the inner contrasexual sooner or later results in depression—the withdrawal of whatever psychic wealth remains to an isolated ego.

When neurosis, or a so-called mid-life crisis, finally strikes, then one can ask why it occurred and turn it into a golden opportunity to contact one's life-giving, whole-making resources. In so doing,

one may turn apparently meaningless suffering into a creative illness. Or, one can reject the opportunity and contract even more
firmly with one's truncation and one-sidedness, thus cheating life
and its basic demand to become whole.

But the difficulty in contracting this inner marriage points even
deeper into the unconscious, to the Great Mother—in Jung's imagery the power of the unconscious itself as it gives birth to the ego
and to whatever consciousness exists. This is the unconscious as
the "matrix mind," the source of all that can become conscious.[7]
When this powerful dimension of the unconscious is in its negative
face it seeks to prevent the development of the ego. Like a devour-
ing mother it tries to consume the ego, to enclose the ego in its
folds, or to begrudge its support as the ego tries to break free. Every
ego that does emerge into the light of consciousness is faced then
with the challenge of reentering the womb from which it came, to
wrest free from a grudging source the energies that contribute to its
second birth and ongoing revitalization.[8]

This is the hero's quest. It means for Jung the search for one's
wholeness by entering a second time or many times into the source
of life and regaining there one's truer fullness. Thus the hero in the
fairy tale returns after his ventures in the forest with, for instance,
a horse, a maiden and a golden bird. He brings renewal to his own
consciousness and through it to the whole kingdom. In this sense
the deepening and extension of the individual's consciousness is
never without a wider social implication. Indeed Jung frequently
makes the point that only the individual is the bearer of meaning
and so of socially significant change, and that such socially
regenerative consciousness must always withstand the engulfing
power of the socially dominant mind set, which Jung calls collective
consciousness.[9]

Only as the inner marriage is consolidated does the mystery of
the Self begin to emerge. As the major paradox in Jung's thought,
the Self appears both as the power that orchestrates the marriage of
the ego with the unconscious and as the child which results from
it.[10] Thus the Self for Jung is that more compendious personality
which emerges as the product of the growing unity between conscious and unconscious. Often it appears as a numinous child, the

divine child, the product of the union of the ego with its inner spouse.[11] Yet the Self is also the power, like the Philosopher's Stone, which was directing the drama from the outset.[12] The Self is therefore both the product and the cause of the union of the ego with the inner man or woman, that is, of the conscious with the unconscious. In this respect Jung's understanding of life's journey toward the Self is not unlike the process described by T.S. Eliot in his famous lines:

> We shall not cease from exploration
> And the end of all our exploring
> Will be to arrive where we started
> And know the place for the first time.[13]

For Jung too the Self is our inner truth, born as a child at the end but bringing together the partners in the marriage—who conceived it in the beginning.

It is particularly in the symbols of the Self, which Jung sees produced universally by the unconscious, that he identifies a process in which the coming into possession of one's complete humanity coincides with the awareness that one's personal experience is continuous with that of mankind.

The movement of the psyche toward this unity is no more dramatically documented in Jung's entire work than in his analysis of the dreams of Wolfgang Pauli, the famous Swiss Nobel prize-winning physicist.[14] In his Terry lectures, published under the title "Psychology and Religion," Jung takes three of the dreams in the course of Pauli's analysis to expose his views on the interrelation of religion and psychology. By briefly recounting these dreams I may provide a sketch of how an analysis might move from stage to stage through the resolution of earlier problems toward an impressive image of the Self with all the above mentioned implications.

The first dream in the series depicts the dreamer entering a Catholic church and observing a religious ceremony which ends with a rather compromising wine party.[15] The dream was preceded in the dream sequence by one in which a gibbon or ape was about to be dismembered, and was followed by one in which animals were becoming human.[16] Jung interprets the church dream as pointing, at least in part, to the dreamer's shying away from his need to

undergo psychic dismemberment in the interest of a deeper integration of his instinctuality and so of a better balanced personality.
Rather than face the rigors pointed to in the previous dream, the
dreamer has apparently toyed with the idea of solving his problems
by returning to the religion of his youth which he had not practiced
in years. In this dream he is told by the unconscious that it is an
unacceptable compromise, an attempt to evade the real suffering he
would have to endure if those sides of his humanity so long neg-
lected were to be accepted into his conscious personality.[17]

This interpretation brings up interesting possibilities of how
religious and psychic reality might relate for Jung. Jung's interpretation here, and significant statements he makes elsewhere, suggest
that where a religion functions to relate one to the unconscious and
to its transformative, balancing and expansive movements, it works
well and should be left undisturbed. But where a religious creed
fails to provide access to the sources of life, then the unconscious
itself operates to do so, though on a more immediate, personal and,
in some sense, more primitive level.[18] At least in this dream
sequence the dreamer is told that the unconscious demand that he
undergo the torture of dismemberment in order to assimilate his
shadow side, the instinctual life he has left unlived, could no longer
be fulfilled through a belated effort to take up again his childhood
religion. For him, in this instance, the way to becoming whole
could no longer be through the external, institutional church.

The next dream in the series again depicts the dreamer entering
a church. But this time the atmosphere in the church is one of
solemnity. The people who enter it are truly recollected. The
dreamer himself finds he has truer concentration. And in this dream
a voice speaks these remarkable words:

> What you are doing is dangerous. Religion is not a tax to be paid
> so that you can rid yourself of the woman's image, for this image
> cannot be got rid of. Woe unto them who use religion as a substitute
> for the other side of the soul's life; they are in error and will be
> accursed. Religion is no substitute; it is to be added to the other
> activities of the soul as the ultimate completion. Out of the fullness
> of life shall you bring forth your religion; only then shall you be
> blessed.[19]

Here the dreamer is clearly told that his effort to live a life away from his anima, the inner woman, is a flight from the fullness of life in both its burdens and joys. A religion which would deny the necessity of the union with the contrasexual would be itself such a flight from life, a maiming, rather than a fulfillment, of the humanity of those who practice it. Obviously the dream here is speaking of the dreamer's need to allow his femininity to complete his humanity, and is condemning an attitude which would deny this completion. But what is the source of the voice which speaks these words?

For Jung it is the voice of the Self. When it speaks the dreamer must listen and yield to its wisdom as though he or she were being addressed by the voice of God. This is the Self as ultimate authority, as that power in the unconscious which works toward the unity of the ego with its latent totality in the depths of the unconscious. The voice of the Self seems to point to some power within us which views the ego from a higher perspective, from the viewpoint of eternity. Moreover, it seems to be able to provide from the sources of the unconscious precisely what each individual ego needs as it moves toward its intended wholeness or completion.

It is as if the Self sees the ego as God sees the individual, and, in the construction of a dream, sends to the individual that personal revelation which leads him or her to a fuller personality and through it to a sense of the continuity of one's individual humanity with humanity as a whole.[20]

This natural movement of the psyche toward the coincidence of the opposites involving individual, universe and God is strikingly brought out in the third piece of unconscious material which Jung introduces into this dream series. In fact it is not a dream but an image, "a sudden visual impression," of a "world clock."[21]

Though it is a complicated image its meaning comes down to this: Two circles, one vertical and one horizontal, share a common center. The horizontal circle is peopled by four small men making up a square within the circle and representing, for Jung, the number of completion. The dynamics of the movement of the circles is such that the vertical circle moves the horizontal. The imagery depicts a three-dimensional mandala. It suggests strongly that the vertical or the divine, and the horizontal or the human, share a common center. Furthermore, in the image the vertical circle pulses or empowers the movement of the horizontal, and in so doing relates the horizontal to its wholeness—to all four corners of the world and so to the created universe itself.

We have here, then, an image of both the completion and the dynamics of that completion to which the psyche naturally moves. The implication of the image is this: as the psyche moves to its center it meets there its relation to the vertical, that is, its relation to the divine which runs through it, and in so doing relates the individual, through his or her experience of an inner divine pulsation, to the movement of the universe—which itself is moved by that same pulsation.

This is the meaning which Jung attributes to that phrase he so often and fondly quotes, and which he takes in part from medieval theology, to the effect that God is a circle whose center is everywhere and whose circumference is nowhere.[22] In human terms, it seems to mean, according to Jung, that in the depths of each life there is a divine center whose circumference is nowhere in the sense that it relates each individual to unbounded growth, to a greater power which encompasses all.

In connection with this center, or in drawing near to it, the individual comes into touch with the divine as center of both his or her being and of all that is, has been, will be and can be, but never in such a way as to lose his or her ego to it. Rather, the rhythm of the approach to this center seems to be the constant death of the ego to subsequent resurrected states of consciousness that progressively approach the divine viewpoint without ever coinciding with it. For these reasons Jung closely relates the Self as the goal of the individuation process to man's nature as the image of God. Just as the image of God unites in the Holy Spirit the opposites of infinite power and infinite meaning, so does the individual come to participate more deeply in this life as the unconscious comes to incarnate itself progressively into consciousness and so give birth to the Self as spirit.

Needless to say, this progressive unification of the opposites of the unconscious and consciousness from which the Self is born as spirit, involves the ongoing suffering of the ego at the hands of the unconscious in the interests of the newly emerging Self. This dialectic of the inner priesthood and victimhood is for Jung the archetypal meaning of the Catholic sacrificial rite of the Mass.[23]

All the major images of the Self that Jung discusses have some religious import. Let me briefly outline a few. We have already seen the mandala, whose religious import is that man's divine center relates him both to his personal wholeness and to cosmic totality. Jung points out that modern mandalas frequently contain human rather than divine figures at their centers. His argument here is not reductive.[24] Rather he seems to be arguing that the unconscious produces in modern consciousness a growing awareness of the dialectical identity of God and man and of the unifying and therapeutic implications of this identity.[25] On this point Jung says explicitly that "the Church," meaning Christianity, is not yet able to admit that "nature unites what she herself has divided."[26] Here Jung clearly means the human and the divine. In fact Jung contends in these and similar passages that the unconscious extends the unity of man and God, limited by Christianity to Christ, to humanity itself as its deepest potentiality and maturational goal.

Another image of the Self which Jung frequently addresses is that of the *anthropos*. Again this image implies that the process of coming into the full possession of one's individual humanity—and particularly in the case of the *anthropos* image, through the integration of the instinctual and the spiritual—brings with it a sense of one's inherence in and continuity with humanity itself. This experience of one's individuality moving into empathic continuity with the human itself, and with the cosmos, could be the archetypal experience that lies behind such disparate mythologies and symbols as 1) the Adam Kadmon of the kabbala, 2) the Pauline cosmic Christ, and 3) the Marxist vision of the individual moving into unity with the being of the species.

A final image of the Self is one that Jung borrows from the alchemists: the image of the consciousness of the individual's continuity with the *unus mundus,* the world of all possibility—the source and ground of all human experience and action. Jung borrows this phrase from Gerhard Dorn, a medieval alchemist; it describes the third stage in a maturational process which Dorn understood alchemically and which Jung interprets psychologically.[27] The anthropology, the conception of human capacities, used by Dorn distinguishes between body, soul and spirit.[28] In the first stage of maturation the soul is extracted from the body and united with the spirit in some sense beyond the body. Jung describes this in terms of dissolution, putrefaction, even death; in alchemical imagery it is often depicted as the flight of the soul from the body. For Jung it is a painful but necessary stage of development. It works to free the soul from a compulsive servitude to forces such as an unbridled instinctuality, which would keep anyone so afflicted in the grip of unconsciousness.[29]

But this is only the first stage. For Jung an unembodied spirituality is never adequate to the human spirit. The soul removed from the body in the interests of its freedom must then be reunited with it. This is the second stage and implies a state in which one fully possesses one's body rather than being possessed by it. In this state of a fully embodied spirit one then meets the demands of life and takes part in it in all its phases.[30]

Only then is the experience pointed to by the symbol of the *unus mundus* approximated. It means that one's individual consciousness comes to live more consistently out of the experience of its continuity with its source, which is at the same time the source of all individuality. Jung describes this source and its relation to the individual in terms that are almost identical to Paul Tillich's, as "the eternal Ground of all empirical being."[31] Jung goes on to relate this experience to that of Philo Judaeus when Philo describes the unity of the microcosm (the individual) with the macrocosm (the totality),[32] and to the experience of Plotinus when Plotinus speculates that all souls may in some sense participate in one soul.[33] Again Jung likens the alchemical experience of the *unus mundus* to the Eastern experience which moves to identify, however dialectically, the individual atman with the universal atman, and the individual with the universal tao.[34]

And so, in whatever idiom he puts it, Jung is clearly saying that the *telos* or the movement of the psyche itself is toward the unification of the individual with the totality of his or her individual humanity. Further, that this unification within the individual comes progressively to coincide with the experience of the individual's continuity with the ground of being itself and so with all that is, can be or will be. Just as no alchemist ever did produce the Philosopher's Stone in all its implications, so no consciousness in its necessary finitude and limitation has ever encompassed the ground of all. Thus Jung writes that "psychic wholeness will never be attained empirically as consciousness is too narrow and too one-sided to comprehend the full inventory of the psyche."[35]

Yet, though it will never be attained empirically, the movement of the psyche to that point in which the personal Self draws near to the universal Self is for Jung the natural movement of the human spirit, which will be satisfied with nothing less. In Jung's mind the psyche's movement toward the conscious and sustained experience of the underlying unity of God, individual and universe seems not only to be a matter for philosophical speculation but is one of psychologically verifiable fact, since all the symbols of the Self, all the symbols of human completion, both imply and demand it. This underlying unity of God, individual and universe, ever there and ready to come into consciousness, is for Jung the ultimate healing fact and therapeutic resource.

From these remarks let me draw a few tentative and speculative conclusions that touch on matters philosophical, theological and psychological.

Jung's model of the psyche rests on the supposition that all human consciousness, all its differentiations and all the disciplines based on these differentiations, emerges from the generative matrix of the collective unconscious. Though Jung—facing the joint hostility of his fellow scientists, who might call him a mystic or worse, and of the religious and theological community, who might suspect him of a reductive psychologism—denied a metaphysical import in his thought, I think his protestations in this matter cannot be sustained.

He certainly seems to enter the field of epistemology and ontology when he claims so repeatedly that all that one can know must be known through the psyche, including the reality of God;[36] again when he scorns the notion that the mind is a *tabula rasa* in the face of the evidence that it is constantly enlivened from within by the seething energies of the archetypes and the plethora of symbols that rise to meet the mind from its own depths;[37] and finally, when he denies that the human knower has access to an Archimedian point, a rock of objectivity, outside of the human psyche.[38] In some of his formulations Jung seems to imply that the very being of the soul is constituted by the images and symbols that pass through it on the way to consciousness.[39] Isn't the possibility that we are and know what we imagine, or what imagines itself through us, one that is fraught with ontological and epistemological consequences? I suspect it is.

Jung's ontology and epistemology is grounded in a subjectivity of such a radical nature that it would relate the being of each individual seat of consciousness to the being of the source of all consciousness, in such a way that the individual's experience of reality, both interior and exterior, is ultimately a function of the individual's relation to the activity of the source of all consciousness within the individual. The teleology attached to this ontology and epistemology would depict the intent of the ground of consciousness so moving into individual seats of consciousness as to lead them to a greater personal wholeness, which at the same time would ultimately bring about an intensified relation to the totality beyond the individual, since the movement to personal completion is sponsored by the ground of the totality.

Because of this radical subjectivity which relates the individual immediately to the ground of life universal, Jung gives to psychology, as the discipline whose business it is to explore this subjectivity, a certain pre-eminence among the disciplines. Thus he cites with apparent approval Nietzsche's somewhat cryptic remark that philosophy and theology become, in modern consciousness, the "ancillae psychologiae"—the handmaidens of psychology.[40] And he does this fully cognizant of the fact that for him psychology, as well as philosophy and theology, remain little more than the subjective confessions of their practitioners.[41]

If there is some truth in these aspects of Jung's thought, then it would seem that the philosophical search for a human and humanizing truth must turn to an examination of the prerational depths from which the conscious mind itself arises. Thus understood, philosophy's search for that wisdom its name proclaims it loves might be an experiential entering into the depths of subjectivity not unlike the analytical process itself. A very valuable by-product of this approach might be a growing conviction on the part of the human mind that all its differentiations and disciplines have a common source. This recognition might serve to relate various efforts of mind more harmoniously one to another, and perhaps diminish the fears and suspicions, if not open warfare, that too often now exist between the various fields of human perception.

Let us turn from the philosophical consequences of Jung's thought to those which his work might have for religious studies. I have already noted that Jung's thought contains within itself an explanation of the genesis of religious experience in all its forms. For Jung, religious experience is made possible in principle through the activation of the immense energies of the archetypes and by the ego's experience of the numinosity clothing the symbols, myths and ritual enactments that proceed from this activation. Thus the world religions and the nightly dream proceed from the same source, one to which each individual has access and which has access to each individual. The dreams are a private revelation which, whether dramatically or gradually, lead the individual into her or his myth. Thus when Jung identifies the practice of religion with the observation of what comes out of the unconscious, he is obviously investing the voice of the unconscious with the weight of the voice of God for the individual.[42]

A further and perhaps even more important contribution which Jung has made to religious thought and theology is his suggestion that a natural theology be built on archetypal psychology.[43] Such a natural theology would work to show the basis of the specific myths and rites, and the dogmatic expressions of any particular religion, in the archetypes, and in so doing ground them in the fabric of the universal human religious spirit. Jung offers this natural theology in the hope that it will serve to remove Christian dogma from the domain of what he terms "sacrosanct unintelligibility," a realm into which it too often falls when it is made the object of a blind, and perhaps blinding, faith.[44] Such a natural theology would also help to free the theologian from the hopeless task of proclaiming "doctrines which nobody understands," with the accompanying demand of "a faith which nobody can manufacture."[45]

The spirit of such a natural theology, with its implicit universalism and the suggestion that now competing religions might need the completion the others could offer, would relieve the various religions of their need to impose their myth on others. Rather they might proffer their varying myths as powerful statements of the human dilemma and the possibilities of its alleviation, which may or may not be of help in illuminating the human condition of those to whom they are offered. Those born into a collective myth in which they find only part or none of their personal myth reflected, might then be freer to search for their life-giving truth elsewhere, or to allow their personal myth to weave itself into their lives directly out of their own sacred depths. Similarly, church leaders might be freer in allowing members of the flock to graze and drink in meadows and fields beyond their direct control.

Not only has Jung proffered such a natural theology and its methodology, he has actually used these tools in his work. Thus he shows how the symbol of the Christian Trinity relates to Trinitarian symbolism as it appears in the history of human consciousness. He points to its abiding truth in the triadic flow of energy in any living process, that is, in the flow between its unconscious source, its realization in the ego and its revitalization and renewal through its connection with its source in the Spirit.[46]

In his work on the Catholic Mass he works to show that the truth of Christ as priest and victim is the truth of the flow of psychic growth as the unconscious sacrifices the ego to the demands of further growth, and the ego becomes then the place of the incarnation of the divine or unconscious—which must, in turn, sacrifice itself to the ego as it enters the confines of finitude.[47] Again he develops a natural theology in support of a Christology which would understand Christ as an image of the Self coming through crucifixion to a resurrected and unbroken unity with the Father, the source of all. "I and the Source are one," is something that the experience of true growth drives every human to say who has undergone its terrifying demands.[48]

What might the response of any believer, Christian or otherwise, be to the Jungian proposition that his or her symbol and myth, the object of faith, come out of the unconscious and describe its natural movements? Can believers accept the not too deeply hidden implications of universalism and relativism that such a perspective would bring to a consideration of religious reality, especially in the face of the claim of any religion to be dealing with a "final" revelation? Will the cry be one of psychologism and reductionism or fear at the discovery that God could be so near? Or does Jung hold out a light as yet only dimly appreciated and infrequently used, but destined to gain wider acceptance in grounding a sense of the inescapability of the religious factor in the life of the human spirit, even though Jung makes that religious factor so intimate a part of nature?

Jung contends that the true Vincentian canon, that which is believed everywhere, by everyone and always, is grounded in the archetypal structure of the unconscious.[49] In the light of this contention, religious orthodoxy might come increasingly to be seen as the orthodoxy of the unconscious. This insight might contain the demand that every particular religion seek always to transcend itself in the assimilation of that which its particularity excludes. But are the religions and their devotees up to it? And if they are not, might not Jung ask them if their limited faiths are not the ultimate sin against the human aspiration toward wholeness and unity? These are some of the questions that force themselves on the mind when it reflects on the full reach of Jung's thought on *homo religiosus*. In the final analysis only time will answer them, but perhaps their very asking can help shape the answer.

Let me finally address psychology as both the study of the psyche and as therapy. Whether in search of psychological truth or therapeutic efficacy, Jung would demand of the psychologist that he or she drive the pursuit beyond or deeper than the levels of consciousness, reason and clarity. To deny the truth of the prerational and/or irrational depths of the human, and the continued power of these levels over our conscious thought and behavior, is to truncate the human and to deny to it the further reaches of its potential for good or evil. Wherever this denial takes place it is a disservice to the truly human; in our century this has become a blatantly dangerous thing to do, standing as we are in the wake of our modern wars and the holocaust.

For Jung the turn inward is, in the final analysis, the only one that confronts the deities and demons that drive us to our heights and depths. And, though they remain or retain a much vaster power than does the ego even when the ego turns to face them, yet in that facing does Jung locate whatever hope the individual and humanity as a whole possess for safety, for balance and for the growth of self-acceptance and acceptance of wider communities moving in the direction of human communion.

The turn inward is itself the source of further questions. First, will our humanity ever become sufficiently convinced of the direction from which the divine and the demonic approach it to meet these forces seriously in its depths, and in so doing lessen their manipulative or compelling power in the interests of a freer and more conscious humanity? Or will the gods continue to be the forces that ground our certitudes, and by extension our society, and the demons continue to be the forces that contradict either or both? And finally, should more of humanity actually take Jung's suggestion and invest more of its energies in the exploration of its interiority, would it find in the unconscious a power that is ultimately benign or hostile to it?

Though Jung often depicts the unconscious as being as ruthless as the most demanding and arbitrary God when its overtures are rejected, I think he saw it as ultimately benign—benign in that it works toward the greater unities that give life to life, the unities of the individual with humanity in its totality, which in the depths of each individual connects with the source of the totality beyond the individual.

But the transpersonal powers that both urge toward these greater unities, and which can turn to destruction when frustrated, are immediately at hand in ourselves and must there be given an ultimate fear and respect. In dealing with them we bargain for our humanity. That is why it would be quite in accord with a Jungian perspective to have carved on the psychological mind, as it peers into the depths of humanity, the words Jung had sculpted over the doorway of his house in Küsnacht: *Vocatus atque non vocatus, Deus aderit,*—"Called or not called, God will be present."

2

Love, Celibacy and the Inner Marriage: Jung and Mechthilde of Magdeburg

From a Jungian perspective, the experience of love in all its forms—sexual, celibate and ultimately universal—is grounded primarily in the inner psychic relation between the ego and the powers that dwell in the unconscious.

More specifically, Jung seems to locate the reality of love in the relationship between the ego and the inner contrasexual archetype, the anima in a man and the animus in a woman. It is this relationship that enables the individual to move to ever more inclusive and extensive spheres of empathy, and eventually to a state of consciousness which draws ever nearer to embracing the totality and to being embraced by it.

I will first elaborate on this idea of interior relationship, which seems so central to Jung's thought and yet is a conception which remains somewhat radical or foreign, even perhaps repulsive, to collective Western consciousness. Then I will allow a medieval mystic, Mechthilde of Magdeburg, to speak as a powerful witness to the experience of the marriage with the inner contrasexual, the animus, as a religious love affair. Finally, I will bring Jung into dialogue with what I present from Mechthilde, through his comments on her work taken from his own *Collected Works*. In this sense the thirteenth century will be brought into conversation with the twentieth.

If this procedure is offensive to historical contextualists, let them take further offense from my endorsement of that position implicit if not explicit in Jung's thought and spirit, namely, that archetypal experience refuses the constraints of time and space, and, to some extent, culture. This would mean that Mechthilde's experiences in the thirteenth century and Jung's in the twentieth proceed from those layers of the collective psyche which transcend the confines of time and space, yet invest these confines with whatever life they have from a position somehow beyond them.

This dialogue across the centuries, then, is not only possible but quite necessary if we are to continue with any hope of success the all-consuming search for life after birth—for that life which enlivens life from its own depths—especially in the face of our current murderous collective consciousness, with its ongoing, truncating certitude that the ego and its powers are both the rulers and the exclusive inhabitants of the psychic domain.

By way of conclusion I will suggest that celibate love may have its only nonpathological justification in the witness it bears to the interior wellsprings of all love. As such it may be a phenomenon which could confirm rather than be in tension with the specific genius and demon of Jung's spirit, which I take to be the priority he gave to the symbolic life and so to the interior life from which the symbols flow.

Let us then turn to a consideration of Jung's thoughts on love. The challenge of speaking to love, and especially to celibate love, from a Jungian perspective is heightened and justified by the fact that celibacy appears to be a transcultural reality practiced not only in certain traditions in the Christian world but in certain Eastern traditions as well.

Following a specifically Jungian instinct and methodology, one would naturally search for the archetypal basis which would ground and motivate such like but unlikely practices in disparate cultures and historical epochs. But since celibacy is understood as a form of love, it is necessary to say a few words on how Jung depicts the reality of love in his psychology. I do this fully aware that Jung, in so late a statement as the latter chapters of *Memories, Dreams and Reflections,* confessed he remained to the end incapable of explaining its mystery. Thus he writes, "In my medical experience as well as in my own life I have again and again been faced with the mystery of love, and have never been able to explain what it is."[1] However, we also know that Jung's first response to the myriad dreams he analysed was to confess that he did not know their meaning. Just as he nevertheless had much to tell us of the meaning of dreams, he may also have much to tell us of the meaning of love.

Jung, as I read him, like most depth psychologists and serious epistemologists, establishes a dialectical connection between two relations, namely, the relation of the ego to an inner world alive with powers that address it from their inner autonomy and so transcendence, and the relation of the ego to the external world equally populated by autonomous peoples and powers. And so the question arises, "Granted that the ego faces two autonomies, those of the internal and external worlds, which relation is of prior importance?"

Perhaps using a term like "dialectical" or some functional equivalent like "reciprocal" is closest to the truth of how these relations relate. But I am of the opinion that in this dialectic Jung gives a pronounced precedence of importance to the ego's relation to the inner world and its archetypal forces. In fact, this bias is so pronounced in Jung that both theoretically and therapeutically he seems to argue that the ego's relation to the external world and to the people and powers met there is but a reflection or projection of psychic equivalents in the inner world.

In terms of personal loves and passions, then, the men and women with whom we fall in love would be compelling externalizations or projections of the ego's inner relationship to the various faces of the anima in the man and the animus in the woman.

If we concede to Jung this priority of the interior, two interesting questions then arise in relation to the possibility of healthy celibacy. Is it possible to lead a healthy psychic and so spiritual life without a relationship to the truth and power of the contrasexual? And secondly, can the relationship to the anima or animus be realized without projecting it onto a person in the external world? I think Jung's position on the first question is obvious and need not delay us. He would deny categorically the possibility of psychic health without an adequate relationship to the contrasexual. Thus whatever meaning nonpathological celibate life might have, it could not, from a Jungian perspective, be divested of a love relationship with the anima or animus.

This answer then brings up the second question. If the relation to the anima-animus is essential to health, can it be realized only in projection, and more, only in the acting out? Certain passages in

Jung would again point to an unqualified "yes" to this question. He seems to affirm that both shadow and the contrasexual can only be perceived in projection when he writes:

> The shadow can be realized only through a relation to a partner, and anima and animus only through a relation to a partner of the opposite sex, because only in such a relation do their projections become operative.[2]

One could hardly ask for a clearer answer. Jung seems to be saying here that only in relation to a person of the same sex with whom we enter into conflictual relations, if he or she be negative shadow, or relations of admiration if he or she be positive shadow, do we come to realize aspects of our own potentiality which cry out for admission into our conscious personality. And, of more importance to our concern here, only in relation to an external partner of the opposite sex can one see reflected the relation to the internal anima or animus.

However, there are other streams in Jung's thought, especially in his sustained interest in the gnostic, mystical and alchemical traditions in both East and West, which would support the contention that the anima or animus might be met and embraced directly in a more immediately psychological and hence spiritual manner.

In what follows I would like to speculate on the further implications of this possibility and to contend that the archetypal truth of celibate love is not that of sexual unrelatedness. Love without some type of sexual component may be a human impossibility. Rather the truth of celibate love may be grounded in a life of progressively more intense intercourse with the inner contrasexual. The true celibate would then be one who moves directly to the relationship with the inner sexual opposite, and through the energies of this union relates creatively to an ever more extensive world beyond his or her individuality.

Regarding this last point, the extension of love that Jung attributes to the further reaches of the individuation process, let us reflect further. For Jung certainly ascribes an immense importance to the inner love affair, understood as the ego's interaction with the anima or animus. Indeed, as noted above, without it he would question or deny the possibility of mature life or love. But in the full range of Jung's thought it is not the most intensive or extensive experience of love. For the union with the anima or animus gives birth to the experience of the Self—and for Jung the experience of the Self cannot be formally distinguished from the experience of God, nor can the images of the Self be distinguished from the images of God as they are formed in, by and through the psyche.

With the emergence of a sense of the Self, there seems to be a corresponding extension of love in the consciousness thus graced. In the case of a man, for instance, as a sense of the Self emerges the anima is seen not only as an individual or actual woman but as the *anima mundi,* the soul of the world, or as Sophia, the consort of the Logos, missing to a large part in contemporary Christianity but playing with and inspiring the Creator at the beginning, and ideally throughout creation. And when the Self emerges in the feminine psyche the loved one becomes, again, more than an image of empirical man. Rather he can become the incarnate God. In the case of Mechthilde, whose imagery I will shortly introduce, he becomes a youthful Christ figure cast in the role of courtly lover, with the power of the Trinity standing in the background.

Thus Jung seems to be describing a process of loving which may begin with images of individual human partners but moves through them to states of consciousness in which all that is perceived is seen as transparent to its divine ground. Jung nowhere describes this consciousness more forcefully or with more beauty than in the latter pages of his major work, *Mysterium Coniunctionis.* There he depicts the culmination of the alchemical process, and, by implication, of individuation itself, as a state in which the adept has moved to a perception of reality through the experienced unity of his or her individual consciousness with what Jung calls "the ground of all empirical being."[3] This state of consciousness, I take it, would be one in which one's individuality is experienced in its dialectical identity with the totality, a state in which the microcosmic and the macrocosmic approach an identity in consciousness.

This experience Jung identifies as symbolized most clearly in the figure of the *anthropos,* the image of human unity, which appears in so many mythologies. Jung saw it in the Jewish Kabbala in the figure of Adam Kadmon. He saw it again in the Pauline Christ, in whom all things have their being and with whom Paul identifies himself. I would add that its most recent appearance may be in the mysticism of the young Karl Marx, possessed by the vision of a final state of consciousness in which the being and activity of each individual coincided with that of the species.

I would now like to show how the interior marriage opening onto universal sympathies, which seems to be so much at the heart of Jung's understanding of the maturational process, finds powerful expression in the thirteenth-century mysticism of Mechthilde of Magdeburg.

Her dates are probably 1210 to 1277. She was a member of the Beguines, a community which today might be described as a lay community of Christians seeking a simpler, more evangelical life style. After Mechthilde's lifetime, in the later thirteenth and early fourteenth centuries, the Beguine movement was associated with certain radical tendencies in the church which were to provoke official disapproval. Mechthilde herself met with some opposition in her own lifetime, possibly due to some of the more radical positions in her one work in our possession. The work is entitled *The Flowing Light of the Godhead*. It remained unknown for almost six centuries, until it was rediscovered in the middle of the nineteenth century in the library of the Benedictine monastery at Einsiedeln, not far from Zürich.

From what is known of her life, largely based upon evidence internal to her one extant text, Mechthilde spent most of it in the simplicity of the Beguine community in Magdeburg, not far from present-day Berlin. Later in life, now as a respected visionary, she moved to a convent in Helfta associated with the Dominicans. By that time she was growing blind and the power of her early experience was declining with her sight. But she seems to have been borne along even then by the memory of its prior intensity.

Most commentators have given to Mechthilde a certain distinction among the medieval mystics who have sung of the mystical marriage and of being brides of Christ. The distinction they afford her, and here Jung joins the common opinion, is the frankly sexual nature of her imagery. What further qualifies her for our discussion

are the occasional but not insignificant references which Jung makes
to her in his *Collected Works*.

In my reading of Mechthilde, two distinct but very closely related
images clearly stand out. The first is her sexual encounter with a
young Christ figure. The second is her entrance into the flow and
light and heat of Trinitarian life through this encounter. I feel that
it is not forcing the thought of either Mechthilde or Jung to see these
themes as analogous to Jung's understanding that the marriage of
the ego with the anima or animus gives rise to a sense of unity with
the source of life and light—in Mechthilde's terms the Trinity, in
Jung's the energies of the Self.

Early in *The Flowing Light of the Godhead* she describes being
wooed and won by the youthful Christ. In a sense the young Christ
initiates the contact. He admits that he has wooed her many days
but only recently heard any response. He seeks to meet her and she
has him say in her manuscript:

> Now I am moved
> I must go to meet her,
> She it is who bears grief and love together,
> In the morning, in the dew is the intimate rapture
> Which first penetrates the soul.[4]

Her senses are depicted as her maids in waiting. They urge their
lady to delay not the meeting with her lover, in these words:

> We have heard a whisper,
> The prince comes to greet thee,
> In the dew and the song of the birds!
> Tarry not, Lady![5]

Clad in the clothing of humility, chastity and holy desire, she
advances into the woods to meet her lover. After some delay the
youth meets her and invites her to dance with him as his chosen.
After the dance, cast in terms of a dance of mutual praise, the Lady
is tired and her consort makes this suggestion:

> Come at midday
> To the shade by the brook
> To the resting place of love
> There thou mayest cool thyself.[6]

But before the final meeting in which she is to be thus cooled and refreshed from the rigors of the dance, she enters into a lengthy dialogue with her senses who now, in a strange reversal, try to dissuade her from the final meeting with her lover and from the consummation of her love.

With a certain discernible haughtiness she initially tells them that she prefers to drink of the "unmingled wine" and so of the intoxication of the divine love. Drinking with and of the divine is another of the images of intensity that run throughout her work. But the senses are not to be so easily dissuaded. Rather they offer her, as pallid substitutes for the consummation she seeks, such things as "virgin chastity," "martyrdom," "the counsel of confessors," "the wisdom of the apostles," and angelic brightness, clarity and love. Mechthilde replies that she appreciates these many noble virtues but that they fall short of what she seeks. As a last resort the senses offer her a share in the maternity of Mary herself. But at that moment Mechthilde is not in a maternal mood. She reveals what her mood is in her reply to this final offer when she says:

> That is childish joy
> To suckle and rock a Babe!
> But I am a full grown Bride
> I must to my lover's side![7]

And to her lover's side she goes, even though the senses admit that they cannot accompany her into the crucible of the final consummation—its intensity is so great. Their final word to her is also their leave-taking. They say:

> So fiery is the glory of the Godhead,
> As thou well knowest—
> . . . .
> Who could abide it, even one hour?[8]

Her answer to this parting shot is interesting not only in terms of her own poetry but also theologically, inasmuch as she affirms that her soul, and, by implication, all souls, are made for such love because they are of the same nature as their divine lover. Listen then to her reply:

> Fish cannot drown in the water,
> Birds cannot sink in the air,
> Gold cannot perish
> In the refiner's fire.
> This has God given to all creatures
> To foster and seek their own nature,
> How then can I withstand mine?
> I must to God—
> My Father through nature,
> My Brother through humanity,
> My Bridegroom through love,
> His am I forever.[9]

And so she enters her lover's chambers, in Jung's terms not unlike a *temenos,* a sacred space. It is described in this way:

> Then the beloved goes into the lover,
> into the secret hiding place of the sinless
> Godhead.... And there, the soul being
> fashioned in the very nature of God, no
> hindrance can come between it and God.[10]

There she meets both her Lord and lover and hears confirmed from his own lips that she had always been his by nature, that only the love between them could endure for eternity and satisfy her deepest longing and desire. In part her lover addresses her in these words:

> Therefore must thou put from thee
> Fear and shame and all outward things
> Only of that of which thou are sensible by nature
> Shalt thou wish to be sensible in Eternity.
> That shall be thy noble longing,
> Thine endless desire,
> And that in My infinite mercy
> I will ever more fulfil.[11]

To this her soul replies:

> Lord, now am I a naked soul
> And Thou a God most glorious!
> Our two-fold intercourse is Love Eternal
> Which can never die.[12]

And then comes the consummation:

> Now comes a blessed stillness
> Welcome to both, He gives Himself to her
> And she to Him
> What shall befall her, the soul knows:
> Therefore am I comforted.[13]

It is difficult to imagine a more intense love or intimacy than Mechthilde describes in the above imagery.

Before we leave her I would like to touch briefly on the second major theme I discern in Mechthilde's experience. That is the soul's participation in the flow, life and light of the Trinity, which runs throughout her work and into which she describes herself as entering through her love-making with the Christ figure. In passing I might here point out that the Christ figure would seem to be, in the passages I have cited, a lover peculiarly gifted in bringing about that unity of chthonic instinct with spirit, two apparently irreconcilable opposites which Jung felt must come together if love is to be whole and entire.

When Mechthilde relates her love to the Triune Godhead, her idiom clearly demands the positing of a need in the Godhead for intercourse with the human and so places a need for creation in God. In this Mechthilde may be sounding the same note struck by Jung in his reflections on the motivation for the incarnation, namely, that God becomes conscious of himself through the painful work of human consciousness differentiating and integrating the wealth and contradictions of its own divine depths.[14] However this may be, the implications of the mutual intimacy which Mechthilde draws between the divine and the human clearly place a need in the Trinity to create the human in order to complete itself through intercourse with the creature, and in so doing to break the sterility of its previous splendid but perhaps boring isolation.

Again Mechthilde's imagery on this is charming because explicit. She depicts the Holy Spirit as sundering the unfruitful self-sufficiency of Trinitarian life:

> Then the Holy Spirit put a plan gently before the Father and struck the Holy Trinity asunder and said, "Lord and Father, I will give

Thee of Thyself, a gentle counsel: We will no longer be unfruitful! We will have a creative Kingdom and make angels after my pattern that they may be one spirit with me; the second spirit shall be man. For that alone is joy which in great love and inconceivable happiness We share with others in Thy presence.[15]

In response to the Spirit the Father considers the suggestion to be excellent. First he confesses the necessity for the creation of humanity and then expands on this initial enthusiasm:

We will become fruitful so that man will love us in return and recognize in some measure our great glory. I will make Myself a Bride who shall greet me with her mouth and wound me with her glance. Then first will love begin.[16]

And of this love with the soul, God, like an impassioned lover, simply cannot have enough. Again Mechthilde shows a refreshing honesty when she writes, "God has enough of all good things save of intercourse with the soul; of that He can never have enough."[17] From her part in responding to this love, Mechthilde too sounds like an earthly lover when she confesses that her love also is insatiable and that, through its expression, she is purified by its passion and made more beautiful by its fervor. She writes, and this is one of the passages Jung cites in his comments on her:

Ah Lord! love me greatly, love me often and long! For the more continuously Thou lovest me, the purer I shall be; the more fervently Thou lovest me, the more lovely I shall be; the longer Thou lovest me the more holy I shall become, even here on earth.[18]

In the same vein she writes elsewhere:

The more He gives her, the more she spends, the more she has. . . . The more the fire burns, the more her light increases. The more love consumes her, the brighter she shines.[19]

And so what begins as a lover's meeting with:

The noble Youth Jesus Christ
Who is still as full of love
As He was at eighteen years[20]

—ends with "the heavenly marriage of the Holy Trinity,"[21] its

embrace described by Mechthilde in these words spoken by the
Godhead in the form of Trinity:

> My Son shall embrace you,
> My Godhead shall permeate you,
> My Holy Spirit shall lead you ever further
> In blissful delight
> According to your will.[22]

Let us turn now from Mechthilde's experience and poetry to
Jung's response to it. No doubt the idea of a spiritual marriage with
the inner Christ would not be interpreted by the medieval mind in
terms of the union of the ego with a powerful animus figure opening
out onto an experience of the Self. But I suggest that Jung's interpre-
tive categories, his hermeneutic if you like, are most adequate to
mediating the meaning of Mechthilde's experience to the modern
mind. As well, a Jungian hermeneutic could serve to validate
Mechthilde's experience by showing how it could be understood as
a profoundly humanizing psychic and spiritual event. In doing this
it would also give us some glimpse of what celibacy might mean
in terms of deriving its value from the inner marriage and from the
energies of the Self.

Jung's first mention of Mechthilde, and one of his most significant, comes in *Symbols of Transformation,* volume 5 of the *Collected
Works.* In its original form this work was central to the break which
was then occurring between Jung and Freud. In it Jung was struggling
to define his position that libido was more than, or could not be
reduced to, simple sexual energy. Rather he was groping for a
conception of psychic energy which preceded all the forms which
energy could take and could appear in any of them. It would be a
form of energy which constantly sought its own renewal. It tended
to depict itself in its own symbolic expressions as moving toward
patterns of wholeness as well as renewal.

Jung held even in this early work that the experience of this
energy in its fullest intensity was the basis in humanity for its
consensus, the so-called *consensus gentium,* that God exists. In
relating this conception of libido to the experience of the divine
Jung writes:

Psychologically, however, God is the name for a complex of ideas grouped round a powerful feeling; the feeling-tone is what really gives the complex its characteristic efficacy, for it represents an emotional tension which can be formulated in terms of energy. The light and fire attributes depict the intensity of the feeling-tone and are therefore expressions for the psychic energy which manifests itself as libido. If one worships God, sun, or fire, one is worshipping intensity and power, in other words the phenomenon of psychic energy as such, the libido.[23]

In the next paragraph Jung returns to the same point and is again explicit:

I am therefore of the opinion that, in general, psychic energy or libido creates the God-image by making use of archetypal patterns, and that man in consequence worships the psychic force active within him as something divine.[24]

This would mean that the experience of libido, in the fuller reaches of its intensity, is the basis for the human experience of the God within. "To carry a God within oneself," notes Jung, "is practically the same as being God oneself."[25]

In this context, then, Jung first mentions Mechthilde as one among a number of Christian mystics who, in singing the praises of God in the imagery of fire, light and love, "honor the energy of the archetype."[26] And here Jung cites the passage I have quoted in which Mechthilde begs to be loved "greatly . . . often and long" by her divine lover. Moreover, argues Jung, this love, this intensity of libido, is so desired that Mechthilde says of herself, in a famous passage again cited by Jung, that for it, "My soul roars with the voice of a hungry lion."[27]

Jung returns to Mechthilde again in volume 7 of the *Collected Works,* in the first of the two essays in which he sought to give some early systematic form to his understanding of the unconscious. Here Jung introduces Mechthilde, in an admittedly passing reference, in conjunction with a case where he came to the conclusion, with the help of a vivid dream from the analysand, that she was unconsciously projecting on to him something of a divine "father-lover."[28] This projection was controlling the transference. Jung worked to have her withdraw the transference, which he here refers to as an "inappropriate love," because it is a love which gives to another what belongs to oneself, in this case one's inner divinity. But the experience of this projection led Jung to reflect on why anyone would project divinity on another, in this telling series of questions:

> Was the urge of the unconscious perhaps only apparently reaching out towards the person, but in a deeper sense towards a god? Could the longing for a god be a *passion* welling up from our darkest, instinctual nature, a passion unswayed by any outside influences, deeper and stronger perhaps than the love for a human person? Or was it perhaps the highest and truest meaning of that inappropriate love we call "transference," a little bit of real *Gottesminne,* that has been lost to consciousness ever since the fifteenth century?[29]

The reference here to *Gottesminne* is to that kind of love of God which Mechthilde describes as permeating her soul and her being in the experiences we have described. Jung refers to her and to this quality of love as "an historical anachronism" and a "medieval curiosity," taking shape before his somewhat startled eyes in his twentieth-century consulting room.[30] By these designations Jung does not mean to dismiss the experience. On the contrary he wants to show that the projection and the experience behind it belong to the structure of the psyche, can appear across the centuries in various forms and, when integrated, bring the ego under the benign and freeing influence of its inner divinity.

Jung helped the woman withdraw the projection and, as its truth became internalized in her own psyche, there occurred a process that Jung describes in these terms:

> I had the privilege of being the only witness during the process of severance. I saw how the transpersonal control-point developed—I cannot call it anything else—a *guiding function* and step by step gathered to itself all the former personal over-valuations; how, with this afflux of energy, it gained influence over the resisting conscious mind without the patient's consciously noticing what was happening.[31]

I understand Jung to be saying here that as she withdrew her projection of divinity onto Jung she came into touch with the divinity of the Self, which then gave fresh energy, relatedness and order to her life. Indeed, Jung writes in his essay on the Mass that the experience of the Self is, when withdrawn from projection, both the most intense experience of divinity possible to humanity and the ultimate ground of one's creative self-assertion. He writes:

> So long as the self is unconscious, it corresponds to Freud's superego and is a source of perpetual moral conflict. If, however, it is withdrawn from projection and is no longer identical with public opinion, then one is truly one's own yea and nay. The self then functions as a union of opposites and thus constitutes the most immediate experience of the Divine which it is psychologically possible to imagine.[32]

In these passages, Jung seems clearly to be drawing a comparison between the experience of his analysand in the twentieth century and Mechthilde's in the thirteenth. The basis of the comparison would be that both were undergoing the experience of energies attached to the Self—depicted in consciously religious imagery by Mechthilde, and unconsciously religious imagery (or religious imagery from the unconscious) in the case of the twentieth-century analysand.

Jung has other interesting remarks to make about Mechthilde's experience and its imagery. Like other commentators he notes that in her imagery the *hieros gamos,* the marriage of the ego with the inner divinity, "approaches the physical sphere in emotional intensity."[33] He explicitly refers to Mechthilde's experience of the inner core (the *medulla*) of the Trinity as that which "corresponds to the self, which is indistinguishable from the God-image."[34] He describes her as projecting "her own feminine Eros upon Christ,"[35] and attributes to her a "quite unabashed Christ-eroticism."[36]

Jung has other references to Mechthilde in his works, but I think these are sufficient to illustrate my point that he considered her passion to be grounded in a very legitimate experience of the marriage with the animus and through it of unity with the Self.

It is worth acknowledging here, however briefly, two other methodological perspectives which have deeply engaged the modern temper and modified the contemporary mind. What would the other Karl, Karl Marx, have to say of Mechthilde's consciousness? I've mentioned that she was a Beguine, a member of a new and to some extent radical form of religious life in the thirteenth century. Scholars relate the origin of this movement and of similar movements of religious ferment in the thirteenth century to the *Frauenfrage* (literally "the woman question")—that is, how society was to assimilate an apparent increase in the number of women unable or unwilling to fit into the more socially accepted and demanded patterns of matrimony or convent. From this perspective, membership in the kind of community to which Mechthilde belonged could be viewed in that cultural context as a meaningful form of liberation from the constriction of socially accepted roles. The liberation it offered, however, retained a traditional religious framework, and so her image of freeing and fulfilling love is both largely religious and largely internal.

Thus a Marxist critique could well suggest that the freedom and fulfillment offered by the Self is, in the final analysis, privatistic and internal and so functions as a flight from reality rather than a commitment to its change beyond oneself.

This critique must be borne in mind, I think, by the Jungian. The rudiments of the answer to it lie, in my opinion, in the relational note that Jung always attaches to an authentic experience of the Self. Thus Jung in his reflections on the major images of the Self argues that its experience heightens the sense of empathy and continuity with reality beyond the individual in whom it occurs, so that such an experience cannot be both authentic and at the same time ultimately solipsistic. Yet at the same time I do feel that one cannot be fully loyal to the spirit of Jung's writings and deny the point he makes so often, namely that creative change in reality beyond oneself can only be a consequence of the transformation of oneself.

If we were to turn from Marx to Freud, what would be said of the experiences of Mechthilde? Would he not reduce her experience to that of repressed sexuality and to the imaginal and fantastic attribution to a phantom divine lover of all that was denied physically? I rather think he would.

I introduce these perspectives to show some awareness of them, to bow to whatever truth they might contain, and to heighten the sense of what is involved in a peculiarly Jungian perspective. I would contend that on the basis of the passages I have read of Jung's response to Mechthilde that he would by no means reduce her consciousness to either socio-economic factors or to repressed sexuality.

Rather he seems insistent and consistent throughout his works in affirming that what Mechthilde and other women mystics encounter in their depth experiences of themselves is the power of the animus rising to embrace their femininity and to lead them into the power of the Self, the experience of which has compelled humanity trans-temporally and transculturally to speak of God.

Jung's psychology would thus seem to be equipped to give an explanation of the meaning of celibacy that few others can, because it takes so seriously the reality and autonomy of those transpersonal powers which exist in the psyche beyond the manipulative grasp of the ego and its limited powers of consciousness and will. In this sense Jung's psychology can invest celibate love with a meaning that very few theologies can, and which any theology of pure consciousness, one which would deny or fail to take seriously the reality of the unconscious, simply cannot.

Understood in Jungian terms the healthy celibate lover would be living out of the immense energies of the inner love affair as a sacrament of the Self and the gateway to an ever more extensive love of reality beyond himself or herself. Where celibate love is not thus understood and experienced, it could actually remove one from the inner sources of invigoration, serving rather those truncating forces which inevitably fill the vacuum left by a severed relation to the anima or animus, namely, depression, lethargy, withdrawal, encapsulation in security systems which at the same time become the object of one's rage, and finally physical illness as the incarnate symbol of the inner wasteland.

I know of few Jungians who have explicitly addressed the phenomenon of celibate love as a variation of love itself. One who has is Helmut Barz, currently the president of the C.G. Jung Institute in Zurich. In his *Selbst-Erfahrung* (Self-Experience), he writes that he knows of those leading celibate lives who are moving toward the Self and individuation, though he confesses that they remain something of a mystery to him.[37] He further confesses that it is a happy mystery even though it constitutes something of an affront to the Jungian model of the psyche and its development. He remarks that in his experience celibates, at least those who have consciously chosen celibacy as a lifestyle out of religious conviction, have difficulty in dealing with shadow and contrasexual material because of the dearth of opportunity for encountering these realities in projection.

Barz seems to take as his final position a qualified appreciation of celibate love even in the face of his confessed inability to fit it easily into his model of the psyche. At one point he remarks that whatever its nature and however it works, there probably are far more celibates than those equipped by nature and disposition to follow someone, say of Mechthilde's fine temper, into the full ardor of the inner adventure and to find fulfillment in it.

Though I am taking a position in some tension with Barz's, inasmuch as I feel Jung's work contains ample evidence of celibate experience like Mechthilde's or say Meister Eckhart's—another of Jung's favorites—which led to very intensely individuated lives, I very much endorse Barz's implication that such lives are of rare beauty.

In this sense Jung's thought can be of help to both those leading lives of consciously chosen celibacy and to those institutions which seek to give it some endorsement. For Jung can show both its archetypal truth which, I suggest again, would lie in the immediate and unprojected experience of the Self while also pointing, as does Barz, to its rarity. Thus Jung's categories could provide, in principle, a perspective capable of psychologically validating the possibility of healthy, humanizing and expansive celibate love, while preserving it from the possibility of institutional exploitation and manipulation.

But in the final analysis these latter considerations are too restricted if they are limited exclusively to the religious field. If celibate love has no archetypal and universal meaning, then it is, like dreams and fairy tales and other revelations, too unlikely and too possibly deviational to warrant further discussion. But if it does have an archetypal meaning, then it also has some kind of significance for all lovers of all times and places.

In my view, the archetypal truth of celibacy lies in the immediate and unprojected experience of the contrasexual, and through it of the Self. In this sense the truth of celibacy would point directly to the truth which I feel differentiates Jung's psychology from others, namely, the precedence he puts on what I have called the interior life and on the ego's cultivation of it through its dialogue with the powers that exist in the unconscious, powers that can support and expand consciousness if embraced, or destroy it and those around it if spurned.

If Jung is right, and so much of the commerce of love is to be found in the relation of the ego to its own depths, then what is acted out externally will always be derivative of the inner relationship, and the quality of the external love affair will mirror the relation to the anima or animus and beyond them to the Self. In this sense distinctions between celibate love and other kinds of love are secondary.

All those who have ever loved with the intensity Mechthilde's imagery expresses will recognize themselves in her poetry, recognize themselves and be reaffirmed, braced in the blessedness of their passion. Mechthilde's love, though probably without a physical partner, may well express the furthest limit of the soul's capacity to endure the fire of love. And where the inner embrace takes place, and the fire of which she speaks burns brightly, that fire itself may consume all differences in the manner of its expression beyond the soul in whom it burns.

3

Jung's Understanding of Mysticism:
Psychological, Theological
and Philosophical Implications

Jung's psychology may be called intrinsically religious, inasmuch as it is organically related in each of its phases to that maturational process he terms individuation, whose *telos* or direction is toward a state of consciousness which can be legitimately described as mystical. "Mystical," in this context, means the conscious experience, admitting various degrees of intensity, of the unification of one's individual being, simultaneously informed by the sense of its continuity with the totality and marked by the expanded empathy such continuity engenders.

This chapter will deal briefly with those foundational elements of Jung's understanding of the psyche in which the religious import of its movement to maturation are most evident. It will then present some of the "master symbols" of the Self, and comment on the profound religious implications which Jung found in these symbols and so in the intent of the psyche which sponsors them. It concludes that Jung's psychology identifies the further reaches of maturity with a state of consciousness which can only be called mystical.

My contention here is that Jung's thought on religion and mysticism implies a latent metaphysic which he not infrequently denied was there. If this metaphysic could be isolated, I believe it could contribute to a more unified vision of the currently disparate and often conflictual worlds of psychology, theology and philosophy. Such a metaphysic and its underlying vision might serve to unify in the individual those legitimate but disparate experiences out of which these disciplines are born, while socially fostering a sense of human solidarity beneath and beyond the current and possibly terminal clash of conflicting absolutes.

Our initial point, then, is that for Jung the psyche is natively religious and moves in accord with its own *telos* to mystical states of consciousness. To make this point one must deal, however briefly, with what Jung meant by religion and how he relates it to mysticism.

Jung's psychology is religious in that it claims to have identified in theory and to engage in practice the agencies universally operative in the generation of religion. He argues consistently throughout his works that the archetypes, those powerful latencies in the collective unconscious, are vested with so great an energy that when they impact on consciousness they submit it to an experience of the numinous, the basis of the human experience of the divine. On this interplay of archetypal energies with consciousness, Jung grounds humanity's universal consent that deity exists, as well as whatever truth may attach to the ontological argument that the experience of God is the only "proof" for God's existence.[1]

Regarding the psychogenesis of religion, Jung argues further that collective religions arise from the matrix of the deeper psyche to compensate collective disorder and imbalance, much in the same sense that dreams address similar problems at the personal level. This means that the world religions and the nightly dream have the same author and serve an analogous function in stabilizing and expanding the consciousness of society and individual. It further implies that dialogue with the dream is dialogue with divinity. This makes the analytic process a sacred process, and is the reason why Jung defined religion as the careful observation of that which proceeds from the unconscious into consciousness, with a certain preference given to the dream. Such observation reveals how the gods and goddesses are acting in one's life at the present time, or, at least, during the last remembered dream.

Passing from his understanding of religion to his closely related understanding of mysticism, Jung defines the mystic as one who has had "a particularly vivid experience of the processes of the collective unconscious."[2] He adds immediately, "Mystical experience is experience of archetypes."[3] In these same passages he confesses that he would have difficulty in distinguishing mystical from archetypal forms.[4] By this I take him to mean that symbols or other forms of archetypal expression bearing a highly numinous charge are at once archetypal, mystical and, needless to say, religious, regardless of the literary genre to which they belong.

Like Henry James, Jung pays tribute to the unmediated nature of mystical experience, that is, to the fact that the mystics personally experience the source from which all religion rises to consciousness. He writes, "We would do well to harbour no illusions in this respect: no understanding by means of words and no imitation can replace actual experience."[5] This intimate experience of the source of religious vitality—as opposed to a purely formal religious observance based, as it often is, on a blind faith devoid of personal experience —leads Jung to say that "only the mystics bring creativity into religion."[6]

By this remark Jung means at least two things. First he means that the mystic, who often stands in a definite tradition and contacts the common source of all religions through adherence to one of them, can bring new life and understanding to the symbols and dogmas of that tradition. This the mystic does through the immediate experience of the living basis of the symbol in the unconscious. There is a sense in which Jung himself did this in his work to retrieve the meaning of major Christian symbols and rites from their state of modern "sacrosanct unintelligibility."[7] Thus, for instance, in his work on the Trinity,[8] the figure of Christ,[9] and the psychology of the Catholic Mass[10] he sought to show how these symbols and rites were expressions of the archetypal movements and energies of the unconscious.

The true function of these energies, according to Jung, is to lead the believer or participant into an immediate experience of the unconscious from which these symbols are themselves born into consciousness. In this role the mystic could revitalize the traditional symbol system by personally experiencing, and leading others into the experience of, the primordial sources of renewal these systems can mediate when not encrusted by the familiarity bred by creed and dogma.

But at a second level Jung implies that the mystic in his or her incursions into the unconscious can discover there elements missing from tradition. In this Jung is simply developing one side of his theory of compensation, according to which the unconscious spontaneously proffers to consciousness what is required for the latter's wholeness. Thus the mystic, with so immediate, intense and sometimes prolonged an experience of the unconscious, may be put in the position of bringing to the tradition the missing wholeness it needs for its own healing.

In this context Jung refers to the mystical experience of Nicholas of Flue, a fellow Swiss, which complemented the reigning male God with that of a Goddess.[11] Likewise Jung valued the mystical experience of Guillaume de Digueville, who saw God as king with earth as queen.[12] To the extent these experiences imply that the collective myth lacks, in the one case, a sense of the divinity of the feminine, and, in the other, a sense of the divinity of matter, such mysticism can become prophetic and urge a broadening of contemporary religious consciousness not infrequently threatening to the collective myth and to the religious tradition which supports it. Thus the suffering of tension with the tradition may attend the mystic's return to the collective, just as it afflicts the hero or heroine in so many fairy tales when they bring back the fruits of their arduous adventures. This means the suffering described in fairy tales and in the stories of the messianic personalities of religion's founders may share much of the same psychodynamic.

These, then, are some of the major definitions, descriptions and implications of Jung's conception of religion and of the primary place of the mystic within it. Let us now locate these reflections within the broader framework of Jung's understanding of the psyche and its movement to maturation.

Individuation, the process of the realization of the Self in consciousness, is central to Jung's psychology and in one way or another touches every aspect of it. Basically the process describes the propulsion of the ego from the unconscious through the agency of the Self and the progressive incarnation of the Self into its own creature, the ego. For Jung the Self presides—though not without the cooperation of the ego at crucial stages—over the whole enterprise. The ego once born from its unconscious matrix becomes the co-author with the Self of the Self's progressive incarnation in the ego.

In individual life this incarnation is most directly achieved by the conversation between the ego and the Self. The latter usually expresses itself most explicitly in the language of the dream. As the intent and attitude of the Self is perceived and then engaged by the ego, the Self is progressively ushered into consciousness, where it becomes a more endemic component of the ego's reality. The authentic coalescence of ego and Self carries with it the sense of a balanced inner order, an enhanced vitality due to a greater access to libidinal energies and an extended embrace or empathy for the surrounding world. In this manner does Jung understand the emergence of that "more compendious personality"[13] or "supraordinate personality,"[14] which comes to birth in every life which suffers the Self's ingression.

The process Jung describes here is admittedly a highly dialectical one. For example, it is true to say that the Self having given birth to the ego seeks its conscious realization *through* the ego. Thus conceived, one can rightly say that the Self from its basis in the unconscious is the creative precedent, the generative source, of the ego, exercising a function not unlike that of the creator in popular Christian imagination. But as the process moves to its culmination, the ego's response to the Self becomes crucial to the Self's birth into consciousness. This is why Jung occasionally refers to the Self as the *filius philosophorum,* the child or son of the ego, born into consciousness through the conscious efforts of the alchemical philosopher to achieve wholeness.[15] In alchemy this process is the *opus,* the work of transformation, whose true gold is the conscious realization of the Self, redeemed from the leaden matter of its unconscious existence.

A further complexity, of interest to the religious mind, which attaches to the dialectic of individuation arises from the organic self-containment of the process. In Jung's psychology one can speak of the unconscious transcending the ego in that the ego can never exhaust nor encompass it. Indeed, Jung describes the unconscious as having no known boundaries and in so doing conjures up images of its infinity.[16] Yet each center of consciousness, each finite ego, remains throughout its existence organically and ontologically related to this sea from which it is born. Processes of individuation thus imply the intrapsychic transcendence of the Self and of the unconscious as such to the ego, but deny the significance of extrapsychic transcendence, such as popular imagination and official theology would attribute to the various one and only Gods of the currently competing monotheisms.

Theologically it is difficult to avoid the conclusion this side of Jung's thought compels, namely, that humanity and divinity are engaged in processes of mutual redemption, in an intimacy so real that it cannot accommodate that conception of divine transcendence which would posit a God ontologically independent of created consciousness or wholly other in relation to it. [17]

The question may then be asked, "Why is the process religious, even mystical?" The most adequate answer is that the process is religious because the collective unconscious, as the generator of consciousness, is the creative ground of all consciousness, and itself seeks to become conscious in human consciousness. To the extent this intent is realized, this common ground imbues each individual center of consciousness with an experience of its inner unification accompanied by a sense of universal relatedness.

The sense of personal completion and extended empathy are for Jung the hallmarks of the Self and of humanity's experience of grace. It is in such experience, and the symbols which it produces and which help produce it, that Jung locates the truth of humanity as an image of God. Of the unity of the individual with the unconscious worked by and incarnate in the Self, Jung writes, "The self then functions as a union of opposites and thus constitutes the most immediate experience of the Divine which it is psychologically possible to imagine." [18]

No doubt in this passage Jung is speaking of a consciousness blessed by a profound experience of the Self. But Jung, read in his totality, must be understood to insist that it is to such harmonies and wholeness that the psyche is driven by its very nature. Thus he describes the direction in which individuation moves as one toward the experience of the near identity of one's personal center with the center of the universe. He writes that the bearer of such consciousness "is . . . of the same essence as the universe, and his own mid-point is its centre." [19]

That Jung considered such consciousness as the goal of the process of individuation, and not as an epiphenomenal or freakish event, is particularly evident in a passage which describes the psychological meaning and functioning of cross imagery. Through the power of such imagery, writes Jung, "the unconscious man is made one with his centre, which is also the centre of the universe, and in this wise the goal of man's salvation and exaltation is reached."[20] Here Jung equates the fuller realization of the Self with that religious and mystical experience of a personal centeredness, grounded in and made possible by the approximation of the ego and its consciousness to the center of the totality within the psyche of each individual. Jung makes it quite clear that this consciousness is at once the *goal* of psychological maturity and the height of religious experience.

Turning now to Jung's discussion of what he considered as master symbols of the Self, it must first be noted that he always emphasized their religious implications. The symbols to be discussed here are the mandala, the *anthropos* and the alchemical process culminating in a sense of the *unus mundus*—the one world—which Jung implicates in the phenomenon of synchronicity. The significance of these symbols has already been addressed in chapter one; here we will approach them from a somewhat different point of view.

Jung was particularly attracted to the mandala as expressive of the sense of the sacred which attached to the experience of the Self. Among its many meanings, Jung saw the mandala as a symbol of the centering power of the Self—its ability to unite the opposites on its periphery in a center which was at once divine and in every psyche. More, this center was such that no ego could totally identify with it and so come to as universal a relatedness and comprehension as an unqualified unity with the center would afford. For Jung this latter occurrence would provoke that psychosis which always follows the soul's falling into the hands of the living God.

Mandala imagery, as Jung interprets it, implies that the ego's attraction for its divine center can neither be evaded nor fully realized. Its attempted evasion would mean the aimlessness of a life uprooted from its sacred depth and center. Yet unqualified unity with the center would mean the loss of the ego's freedom to a destructive identity with its divine ground. Indeed, it is this near lust for its sacred origin that prompts Jung to point to the dangers faced by the ego on the journey inward, where the experience of the renewing vitalities of the unconscious can consume as well as revitalize. In their experience of these depths the mystic, the addict and the fanatic are equally aware of their possessive allure.[21] Only

the mystic redeems the experience by bringing it back to consciousness in the service of humanity.

Jung found much of the religious truth of the mandala expressed
in the saying referred to earlier, that God is a circle whose center
is everywhere and whose circumference is nowhere.[22] This meant
for Jung that God is the center and centering power in each psyche,
though no individual consciousness could ever exhaustively encompass the circumference or the totality of all that emanates from the
center in created reality. Again this would mean an unqualified unity
with the center, which would consume the ego.

Let us leave this image with the observation that for Jung the
closer the ego draws to its divine center, the source of all created
opposites, the better can the ego relate to the opposites in its own
inner life as the basis for a better relatedness to them in external
life. This dynamic may lie at the heart of what is often said about
the mystical journey, namely, that the journey inward is the journey
outward. This would imply that the mystic's inner achievement is
never without social consequence, which may explain why mystics
who have achieved some high degree of the union of opposites
within themselves may then become vehicles of resolution of social
and political conflicts beyond themselves.

The symbol of the *anthropos* picks up this social implication of
mystical consciousness. It too rests on the experience of the unification of one's disparate personal energies together with an extended
sympathy, but with a heightened sense of the coincidence of one's
individuality with universal humanity.[23] In such images as the Jewish
Adam Kadmon, the Pauline cosmic Christ and the gnostic experience
of an inner and universal Christ, Jung sees variants on the theme
that one's humanity in its depth is at one with the humanity of others.

With the demise of specifically religious myth and symbol in
contemporary consciousness, one might wonder with Jung if the
anthropos archetype and the kind of *participation mystique* it engenders in the construction of community has not passed into the political
realm. Here it functions to imbue its adherents with a sense of
alignment with an historical process which necessarily moves toward
a community of communion as the goal of history. Such a vision
seems to have enlivened the thought of the young Marx. This is

most evident when he describes a consciousness that would inform its holders with a sense of the species, which in turn would generate spontaneous activity on behalf of humanity itself as it moved toward its final union of communion. Thus because of their power to render the communities they create relatively unconscious, Jung points consistently to the social and political dangers which attach to the very same archetypal energies which empower mystical consciousness.

In my opinion, the mystical and religious implications of the Self are nowhere so well, one might even say methodically, developed as they are in Jung's discussion of the three-stage process leading to the state of consciousness called the *unus mundus,* the one world. His reflections on this process come at the end of his last major work, *Mysterium Coniunctionis,* and serve as a capstone to the work of his lifetime.[24]

The term *unus mundus* is taken from Gerhard Dorn, a late medieval alchemist. In appropriating the process Dorn describes, Jung accepts Dorn's anthropology, which divides the human into the realms of body, soul and spirit. Again following Dorn, Jung describes an initial psychic ascetic stage whose culmination is symbolically depicted as the separation of the soul from the body—a state Jung interprets to mean a freedom from the constrictive powers of instinctual and destabilizing emotionality.[25]

This first stage brings the soul before what Jung calls "the window into eternity."[26] But because Jung's psychology moves from this ascetic stage back into embodiment, it does not allow the soul to step prematurely through this window and away from the confines of finitude. In one of the more radical points in his critique of Christianity, Jung argues that this preliminary and ascetic stage of psycho-spiritual development is as far as Christian spirituality extends. Thus he criticizes official Christian theology for its rejection of a pantheism which would support the sense of the divinity of matter and body. He writes, "And although it was also said of God that the world is his physical manifestation, this pantheistic view was rejected by the Church, for 'God is Spirit' and the very reverse of matter."[27]

Jung goes on to attribute this pathologizing removal of the sense of divinity from the physical and incarnate human to the central figure in the Christian myth, in these words: "Despite all assurances to the contrary Christ is not a unifying factor but a dividing 'sword' which sunders the spiritual man from the physical."[28]

In Jung's reading of Dorn the alchemist, this unincarnated spirituality demanded reincarnation if it was to serve the whole person, which would have to include the embodied person in relation to the world. Hence beyond this first stage there is a second in which the soul, united with the spirit and so freed from the compulsions of the body, is reincarnated to effect a spiritualized body or an embodied unity of spirit and soul. Jung writes, "By sublimating matter, he [the alchemist] concretized spirit."[29] The alchemists described this state of consciousness as a *caelum*,[30] a heaven, in which body, soul and spirit become one. They also related this state to what they called the glorified body, and, Jung suggests, may have understood it to be an experiential equivalent to the resurrection, implying some temporal anticipation of resurrected consciousness.[31]

From this state of a unified personal being firmly embodied in space and time, the process moves to a third and final stage: the extension of empathy toward an embrace of the whole, through unity with the source of all in the ground of one's being. This stage is best described in Jung's own terms as he adapts Dorn to his psychology. He writes, "For him [Dorn] the third and highest degree of conjunction was the union of the whole man with the *unus mundus*."[32]

To get at what is involved in the unity of the whole person with the *unus mundus,* Jung draws an analogy with the symbol of the "one day" taken from Bonaventure's *Itinerarium*. Jung understands this day to be the first day of creation and he equates the consciousness of this first day with the consciousness Dorn seeks to describe with the term *unus mundus*.[33] "By this," writes Jung, "he meant . . . the potential world of the first day of creation, when nothing was yet 'in actu,' i.e., divided into two and many, but was still one."[34] For Bonaventure this world of the one day refers in symbolic terms to a state "prior to the fall," when creation was fully at one with and transparent to its divine ground. In orthodox theology this describes a prelapsarian state of consciousness which will be recovered in a post-temporal eschaton when God will be all in all.

The amazing claim that Jung is here making in his reading of Dorn is that this consciousness is the goal of the transformation toward which the process of individuation and its alchemical catalyst naturally work. It is an experience which is accessible to and even demanded of a maturing consciousness in time and space. Jung obviously means this when he writes of the alchemical endeavor:

> The creation of unity by a magical procedure meant the possibility of effecting a union with the world—not with the world of multiplicity as we see it but with a potential world, the eternal Ground of all empirical being, just as the self is the ground and origin of the individual personality, past, present, and future.[35]

In the context, Jung understands this union with the ground of being to take place only in a consciousness fully embodied in the conditions of finitude.

In this passage Jung clearly affirms that the psyche is driven by its own *telos* toward that consciousness which the Christian myth locates in the past—in Eden—and in the future—the New Jerusalem—but hesitates to describe as a state of consciousness to be realized in the present as the culmination of the psyche's natural maturation. The implications of this consciousness are made evident in the examples Jung chooses to amplify it. He sees such consciousness depicted in Philo's conception of the individual as a microcosm who realizes consciously "the unity of the psychic man with the cosmos."[36] He sees it in Plotinus's speculation that "all individuals are merely one soul."[37] He sees it again reflected in Eastern thought when he describes it as "the relation or identity of the personal with the suprapersonal atman, and of the individual tao with the universal tao."[38]

Perhaps the most significant amplification of the *unus mundus* is in the manner Jung relates it to other master themes in his own work. He writes, "If mandala symbolism is the psychological equivalent of the *unus mundus*, then synchronicity is its parapsychological equivalent."[39] This remark provokes the question, "What do the *unus mundus,* the mandala and synchronicity have in common?"

As we have seen, the mandala for Jung points to the universal presence of the divine in the center of each psyche as its ultimate point of consistency, working internally to draw consciousness into its stabilizing influence and so to relate consciousness more adequately to the external world. The experience of the *unus mundus* harmonizes with the imagery of the mandala because it too points to the presence of the ground of being in each existent psyche, implying that the movement of the psyche is toward the ego's conscious union with this ground and so with the totality which this ground also sponsors.

Synchronicity as understood by Jung presupposes a common generative substrate giving rise to all centers of consciousness and indeed to non- or pre-human nature.[40] But with synchronicity Jung introduces the added note that this common ground can, in effect, intervene in consciousness, usually under stress related to the deeper truth each life seeks. In discrete synchronistic episodes, this substrate dramatically orchestrates events between individuals or between individuals and nature. The individual is so impressed by striking "meaningful coincidence" that his or her consequent life is transformed toward the realization of its deeper truth conveyed by the sense of the event. What can with every justification be dismissed as pure chance by the disengaged observer is perceived as a "providential" intervention in the life which it touches.

The wealth of such events in his life and in the lives of his patients eventually forced Jung to the conclusion that each center of consciousness continues in its finitude to participate in its pre-finite or eternal ground, and that its ground could intervene in certain lives to work patterns of meaning in defiance of all statistical probability. More than this, he believed that this ground was inextricably connected with finite consciousness, which in one sense is its product and in another the place where this ground seeks its fullest realization. Further, its wisdom manifest in the synchronistic event implies a viewpoint superior to that of the stressed ego it addresses. Indeed this ground can convey its wisdom on occasion through the orchestration of external events, both human and natural, with a dramatic impact surpassing even that of the dream which manifests the same wisdom internally.

But more important than discrete synchronistic events is the synchronous consciousness they point to and whose appropriation they in some sense urge. Such a synchronous consciousness would be characterized by a residual sense of its possessor's rootedness in the ground of the universe, with the resultant heightened capacity to perceive the sacred in all else as similarly grounded. Though intermittent synchronistic events may aid the traveler toward this awareness, such consciousness as a residual state seems to be the goal to which the psyche moves with all of its energies.

One must assume that Jung took this description of the movement of the psyche toward its maturation to be in some sense based on the nature of the psyche, and so, allowing for immense variations of cultural expression, a universal process in which every psyche participates. The process he describes as individuation is not atypical, epiphenomenal nor confined to a privileged few. Yet it is equally clear that this process moves inexorably toward patterns of individual wholeness in tandem with a more universal empathy which Jung equates with the experience of grace and of God, though such experience is a work of nature and nature's goal.

In so conceiving of the psyche, Jung identifies psychological maturation with the further reaches of religious and mystical experience. Thus the goal toward which individuation moves is a state of consciousness which unites the psychological, the mystical and the religious—a unity which continues to surpass most modes of contemporary perception and all too often the self-understanding of those engaged formally in the disciplines of psychology and religious studies.

More than this, Jung's understanding of the psyche raises the issue of a surreptitious metaphysic operative throughout his psychology. Though Jung is frequently heard to deny the status of metaphysician to the psychologist, and to himself as a psychologist, he obviously enters the metaphysical realm when he argues that whatever is known is known through the psyche and that existence itself is psychic.[41] Further, there would seem to be metaphysical implications when he dismisses as naive the Aristotelian and Thomistic claim that there is nothing in the intellect except what comes in through the senses.[42] To the contrary, Jung would claim that the psyche is alive with the God-creating energies of the archetype even as a precedent to its creation of consciousness, and that these powers continue their semiautonomy even after the creation of consciousness and its consequent fascination with the sensible world.

In addition, Jung seems to give psychology itself a certain supremacy in the world of metaphysics, and indeed of all the human disciplines, when he argues that even metaphysical statements are statements of the psyche and so are themselves psychological reflections of the complex or complexes dominant in the philosopher's or metaphysician's psyche.[43]

These are metaphysical claims of the first order which justify the attempt to isolate the metaphysic that is there. Its rudiments may be as follows: All that is significantly knowable, as well as the possibility of consciousness itself, exists originally in what Jung calls the "matrix" nature of the creative unconscious,[44] the source of all consciousness but in itself wholly undifferentiated. As consciousness proceeds from this seething precedent, it becomes the agent which first perceives, then differentiates and finally reunites the antinomies and contradictions of its unconscious generator.

Dialectically this process is initiated and presided over by the Self. The Self seeks conscious realization in individual lives through first constellating and then reuniting opposites in human consciousness which remain contaminated or undifferentiated in the unconscious. The philosophy of history and, religiously, the eschatology consistent with this metaphysic, is one in which archetypally empowered opposites, usually concretized in communities of conflict, move to their resolution in more inclusive syntheses. On this point Jung may be closer to Hegel than he himself was aware till very late in life.[45]

When this metaphysic is given its theological formulation, Jung is found to be arguing that God seeks through human consciousness a unity of opposites which defied realization within the Godhead. This ultimately is what demands the creation of consciousness, and forces Jung from a trinitarian to a quaternitarian paradigm. In this paradigm the creative but unconscious One differentiates into its opposites in historical consciousness, and then brings the opposites together in the age of the Spirit.

The moral imperative arising out of this metaphysic and its theological equivalent demands that the individual, with the help of the Self or of deity, bring to consciousness and then hopefully to some resolution whatever form of the divine self-contradiction is most operative in that individual's life. In this manner are God and the human dimly aware of their ontological bond from the outset, both engaged in mutual redemption in history.

In the final analysis, the philosophical and theological conse-quences of this paradigm significantly undermine current religious configurations of transcendental monotheisms, as well as equivalent absolute monomyths in the political order. Jung's paradigm grants to them all a relative truth based on their archetypal grounding. But it denies to them any finality. In Jung's psychological reflections on twentieth-century political "isms," he argues that the lust for the absolute and its certitude has moved into political configurations, aided to a great extent by religion's theological self-discrediting in its conversation with modernity. Collective humanity is now com-ing to see that its hope for the future is increasingly dependent on the sacrifice of its current faiths, political or religious, to a broader human sympathy than they can apparently mediate.

Since these faiths owe their origins to the unconscious, and since the mystic has some ready access to it, the fostering of such sensitiv-ity, whether it be done by specifically religious or psychological agencies, may make a significant contribution to the emergence of a broader and more encompassing empathy. This newer sense of our common humanity, at one in its origin and in the common task of the hazardous historical redemption of its origin, may in the end provide an unlikely but powerful alternative to our possibly immi-nent destruction at the hands of lesser, still competing, gods.

4

Psyche and Theos:
Jung and Tillich Reconsidered

This chapter will develop around three major points. First it will simply urge that the correlation of the worlds of Christian theology with psychology has today the same importance as it had for Tillich and Jung in their day. This correlation derives its significance from the kind of question it seeks to resolve. This question can be stated in many ways. In general terms it might be put in this form, "How does religious and more specifically Christian experience relate to the experience of the psyche?" But in a more personally engaging form it could be asked, "Can the Christian be psychologically mature, that is, fully responsible to the psyche's deepest maturational intent and demand and, if so, how so?"

Secondly I will argue that only a theology like Tillich's, equipped with a panentheistic ontology of divine immanence, whose epistemic consequence grounds in humanity's self-consciousness an immediate sense of God, can establish an organic, unforced and so honest connection between the domains of religious and psychic experience. In the final analysis, Tillich's theology does this by making obvious that the experience of theos and psyche cannot be distinguished from the human vantage point.

Thirdly, I will go on to suggest that in their efforts to reconnect the worlds of religious and psychic experience, Tillich's success, possibly as great as a Christian theologian's can be, was finally overshadowed by Jung's for two reasons. Jung was free of the constraints that must impede a mind dedicated to theologizing in the service of an institution claiming possession of or by a final revelation. In addition, Jung allowed himself to have, or had forced upon him, a more intensely personal and prolonged experience of the psyche than was the case with Tillich, who more than once expressed appreciation of the analytic process but never submitted seriously to a personal analysis.[1]

The chapter will conclude that Jung in thus surpassing Tillich authored a myth with an attendant metaphysic which at once appreciates, transcends and so ultimately undermines the Christian myth. In doing this Jung points to a yet unrealized religiosity more capable of honoring the totality of the human individual and of engendering a more encompassing empathy for the totality beyond the individual.

This is the case because Jung's myth is a variant of microcosm-macrocosm thinking, muted if not lost in the West with the demise of the Platonic tradition. In self-conscious continuity with this tradition, especially in his later alchemical works, Jung argues that the natural process of individuation moves of its own nature to patterns of personal wholeness which at once carry with them a wider embrace of reality beyond the individual. In his understanding of the consciousness that attaches to the alchemical conception of the *unus mundus,* Jung is explicit in describing mature consciousness as moving toward a state in which it perceives all that it perceives as grounded in the divine because of its own conscious inhesion in that ground.[2] This indeed sounds like Tillich. Where Jung goes beyond is in describing this state of consciousness as the natural culmination of psychological maturity, demanded and ultimately enabled by the power of the psyche itself.

Further Jung would argue that the commerce between consciousness and the energies which give it birth and urge its maturation is ontologically one of mutual redemption. Theologically, Jung's paradigm necessitates the creation of human consciousness and history as the only locus in which primordial divine instability can seek and hopefully achieve its resolution. Psychological maturation thus conceived becomes itself a sacred reality, what Jung calls the *opus.* In this work which is the challenge at the heart of every life, God is redeemed from the matter of divine unconsciousness, and the human in whom it happens is graced with the experience of the resolution of whatever forms of divine antipathies were operative (as conflict) within that psyche.

This consciousness is not unlike the orthodox understanding of the experience of the Holy Spirit as that power which works the coincidence of opposites, healing the divided individual even as it breeds a more extended empathy for all that is. The burning question between depth psychologist and theologian becomes the question of the authorship of these harmonies and the relationship of the author to the consciousness thus graced. A psychologist like Jung is happy with an intrapsychic model which would establish an intimate bond between the gracing agency and the consciousness graced—indeed, so intimate a bond that the process is one between distinct poles in a unified and organic system. The theologian, on the other hand, must hold out for some form of divine transcendence which addresses humanity out of its freedom and so in a somewhat arbitrary sense. Though Tillich has muted the heteronomy involved in this process with his profound ontology of divine immanence, he cannot, finally, establish either the intimacy between the divine and the human nor their mutual need that Jung achieves in his mature thought.

Let us turn now to our first point, the continued importance of establishing the psyche-theos correlation itself. Both Tillich and Jung felt that the relating of faith, especially in the form of ecclesial, creedal and dogmatic formulations, to psychological maturation was crucial if the believer's psychological development was not to be maimed or even destroyed by the demands of an allegedly saving faith. Tillich will refer to individuals, by implication often the more spiritually sensitive, who are broken in their "personal center"[3] by the apparent need to assent in faith to a body of revealed truths usually taken literally but vested with what Jung has called "sacrosanct unintelligibility."[4]

In his lifelong fight against conceptions of faith which would turn their victims against legitimate sides of their humanity, Tillich argued consistently that a faith experience which did not grasp and engage the individual's totality, including what he calls the collective unconscious, would itself be rejected by the truth of that side of humanity it could not include.[5] Here Tillich provides an adequate description of the psychodynamics of religion as neurosis, for he is depicting a faith which splits the believer between the demands of God to believe and of the psyche to become whole.

Much the same concern to relate the demands of faith to the demands of the psyche is evident in his critique of kerygmatic theology. With its heteronomous presuppositions it would imagine revelation as a stone thrown by a transcendent stone-thrower, or by his earthly proclaimer, at the heads of those who for some reason are to be grateful for this divine attack on their humanity.[6] Against such a divine stranger and his questionable intrusions into the human realm, Tillich more than once suggests that atheism is the most adequate and religious response.[7] These concerns lay behind his constant search for an adequate *vermittlungslehre,* in effect a natural theology which would mediate and humanize the commerce between divinity and humanity.

In his *Systematic Theology* this search bore fruit in his conception of theonomy.[8] With this concept Tillich can argue consistently and cogently that a God not intrinsic to the structures of human being and reason could not reveal through these structures without destroying them. Such revelation, he argues, "dehumanizes man and demonizes God."[9] In all of this Tillich is arguing that a God who does not approach consciousness from its natively sacred depths cannot approach it at all in a nondestructive manner. On this conception of a radical immanence with its panentheistic ontology and epistemology, the bedrock of Tillich's system which makes it forever incompatible with Barth's, Jung explicitly agrees. He too contends that the "wholly other God" can have no happy commerce with the human: "It is therefore psychologically quite unthinkable for God to be simply the 'wholly other,' for a 'wholly other' could never be one of the soul's deepest and closest intimacies—which is precisely what God is."[10]

For Jung, too, had observed at first hand the disastrous consequences of a God wholly external to the psyche in the psychospiritual destruction of his minister father. In Jung's opinion his father's lifelong struggle was with a God extrinsic to the psyche who severed him from the psyche's life-giving libido, and having thus betrayed him, contributed to his depressed and shortened life.[11] One may well argue that *Memories, Dreams, Reflections* is simply Jung's autobiographical myth and that his depiction there of his father's spirituality is part of that myth. But this only worsens the indictment. For Jung's myth about his father is one which moves easily to equate his father's plight with the spiritual plight of our age. Jung diagnoses this plight as a consequence of a transcendentalism which placed, in his quaint phraseology, "all God outside,"[12] and which scorned as "morbid mysticism"[13] the organic connection which Jung sought to establish between religious experience and the deeper experience of the psyche itself.

Thus for Jung and Tillich an adequate correlation of psyche and theos was and remains more than idle speculation or mere play of ideas. It involved the crucial matter of integrating the religious dimension of life with life's maturational demand. The price of failure pitted religion against maturity in a conflict that always resulted in spiritual diminishment or death, which not infrequently becomes physical.

In the light of developments since their time, it is obvious that this problem is still with the Christian mind. After a brief flurry of freedom during Vatican II, Roman Christianity has returned to its traditional authoritarianism, in tension with liberation theology proposing collective solutions to even personal problems in accord with its Marxist inspiration.

Reformed theology seems still fixated in its peculiar form of subservience to a revealed Word held as definitive. This is not to deny the complex scholarship and philology which attaches to this fixation. In their respective penchants for collective consciousness and activity, on one hand, and for a final Word spoken from beyond humanity, on the other, neither side of the Christian tradition seems willing or able to face the depths of their common humanity from which, Tillich and Jung would agree, religion itself springs into consciousness. To do so would threaten the collective mind and possibly unnerve it in its communitarian action and instinct. Such introspection would also undermine the kind of transcendentalism which would give privileges in history, or, indeed, create history, on behalf of the hearers of the One True Word. Hence the psychological suffering attached to belief patterns which alienate the believer from nature's search for wholeness continues. But the question of a more adequate relation of the psyche to deity, the answer to which could alleviate the suffering of those whose humanity is truncated by their religion, is rarely asked or pursued in earnest.

Let us briefly present Tillich's theological answer to this problem, with the presupposition that it continues to hold out to Christian theologians the only possibility of bridging the continued gulf between the worlds of psychology and theology—even if Christian timidity about such bridging has currently turned theological efforts in other directions.

The key to Tillich's correlation of psyche and theos lies in his understanding of essence and existence, which he calls the backbone of theological thought to be elaborated throughout his entire system.[14] Tillich tends to associate essence with all modes of form and so of the defined which can take on connotations of normative reality and so of the good.[15] He further associates it with reason, since reason is the structure of the mind which enables it to perceive structure beyond the mind.[16] Here Tillich holds reason in tension with that which precedes it, though for Tillich essential reason ideally would be wholly transparent to its prerational and sacred depths.[17] For Tillich the full realization of this transparency remains an eschatological conception.

These many meanings of essence are unified around Tillich's conviction that essence in its pristine expression is the ultimate being, truth and goodness of every existent, because essence both universally and individually is expressed initially in the divine Logos as God's self-definition within the dynamics of the Godhead.[18] In this manner Tillich's conception of the essential implicates his Trinitarian theology. Furthermore it is on this understanding of essence as it proceeds from its Trinitarian basis into existence that Tillich grounds the panentheistic ontology and epistemology which supports his sytem and necessitates humanity's universal sense of God.[19] For humanity in existence is never divested of its essential connection with its origin and so is haunted by its longing for that from which it is removed but cannot, of its own accord, regain.

In this way does Tillich capture in concept and language humanity's plight, which can be equally well expressed in philosophical, theological or psychological idiom because the experience of separation from the essential, and lust for it, is, according to Tillich, humanity's most basic experience of itself. Since the essential self is first expressed in the Trinitarian process, Tillich can argue that humanity's native intuition of deity is naturally Trinitarian since it is based on the experience of the unity of divine power and meaning worked by the Spirit.[20] Tillich's grounding of the essential self in the Trinity further implies that recovery of one's essential self involves a fuller inhesion in the flow of Trinitarian life. Such a blessed consciousness would progressively come to live out of its eternal expression within the Trinity, while still within the confines of time. A further consequence of this expression of the eternal now would be a fuller participation in the unities worked by the Spirit within the Trinity.

The Trinitarian paradigm involved in the recovery of the essential self is not unlike central features in Jung's discussion of the Trinity. Jung understood the Trinity to be a symbol based on the experience of the self-renewing power of the psyche. Hence he would relate the generation of the Son by the Father to that of the ego by the unconscious. The renewing energies of the Self, just as the Spirit in Trinitarian thought, then unite these sundered opposites.[21] Thus the Self is both the author and the child born of their union. But, even here, Jung, in effect, as will be discussed later, is making human consciousness the "second moment" in Trinitarian development.

To return to Tillich, his theological integration of the realms of psyche and theos through the interplay of essence and existence is again marvelously evident in his creation-fall theology. Here Tillich continues his reasoning that the Logos, in defining the divine abyss, is the initial expression of the essential. Then he suggests that this initial expression within the Trinity is preliminary, not fully realized, somehow afflicted with a dreaming innocence, an unactualized potentiality which calls for a second creation, the one in which we are currently involved.[22] Second creation is thus the ecstasy or propulsion of essence from its Trinitarian matrix into its inevitable, universal, yet freely incurred distortion in existence.

In their basic descriptions of the procession of essence into existence, Tillich contends that Platonism and Christianity coincide.[23] In a masterpiece of psychotheology, Tillich so conceives of the "fall" of essence into its existential distortion that from the divine viewpoint it describes creation and fall, and from the human viewpoint it describes the human option taken universally and freely to affirm one's existence and in so doing to depart from an unqualified unity with one's essential self, that is, with one's primordial and unambiguous inherence in the Trinitarian life process. Thus the original sin repeated in each life is that of willing one's individual existence and consciousness.[24]

This position is again very close to Jung's description of the problematic need of the ego to be born into consciousness beyond the unconscious and then to reunite with its source in a process of mutual redemption.

Tillich claims to avoid two obvious heterodox implications which would seem to attach to this position. The first would be that the Trinitarian Godhead is forced to create beyond itself because of some deficiency in its creative self-definition. The second is that the creator, regardless of motivation, could not create a perfect world because the very process of human maturation demands severance from the essential connectedness with God in the original sin of willing one's conscious individuality in existence. To avoid implying that the Trinitarian creator was forced to create a fallen world, Tillich save the day and orthodoxy by describing the transition from essence to existence as simply "an original fact,"[25] "a leap" and "a story to be told."[26] It becomes the one place in his system where he not only tolerates but embraces the irrational as the category most adequate to the complexities of the situation.[27]

However questionable his squaring of his understanding of creation and fall within Christian orthodoxy may be, its psychological perspicuity cannot be denied. For it enables Tillich convincingly to argue that existential consciousness is never divested of its sense of connectedness with its essential self eternally grounded in the Logos. Thus understood, life becomes naturally imbued with the quest for the essential self, and so is in its depths sacred and holy. Tillich can therefore give a specifically psychological cogency to his conception of life itself as a religious quest for the essential by contending that this quest or question engages everyone experientially as the genesis of faith universally. In this context he has every right to use the psychological phraseology he does in describing the energy and the goal of this universal quest as ultimate concern.

These same categories enable him to give an experiential and so psychological content to the recovery of one's essential self, which for Tillich is identical with the process of salvation. Thus he will describe life's universal negators as death, guilt and meaningless-ness, and go on to show how the appropriation of one's essential self negates death in the experience of the eternal now, guilt in the experience of one's acceptability in the face of one's unacceptabil-ity, and meaninglessness in the experience of one's essential being in the being and life of God.[28] More than this, he can build an experiential theology of the individual's integration in the face of the threat of the disintegration of life's opposites (Tillich's "ontolog-ical elements"), those antinomies whose union gives harmony to life and whose fragmentation sunders life into destructive one-sided-ness.[29] He does this by showing how a Spirit-worked inhesion in the ground of being is at the same time identical with immersion in the balanced flow of Trinitarian life,[30] fragmentary now but moving of its own dynamic toward an unambiguous eschatological realiza-tion in the process he calls essentialization.[31]

Turning for a moment to the practical, even clinical level, the organicity Tillich establishes between the religious and psychic dimensions of humanity is evident in the way he relates the healing which is proper to salvation to therapeutic healing. This question surfaces most clearly in his discussion of anxiety.

Tillich distinguishes two forms of anxiety: existential, and pathological or neurotic.[32] Existential anxiety attaches to existential and finite life universally and is a function of its distance from essence. It can only be alleviated through the recovery of the essen-tial, which for Tillich remains always a work of grace. In the medi-ation of the essential Tillich locates the legitimacy of the religious or ministerial role.[33] Neurotic anxiety, on the other hand, results from the betrayal of the essential self in flight from life's ever-pre-sent negativities. The alleviation of this latter condition constituted for Tillich the legitimate area of operation for the therapist.[34]

In this way Tillich can theoretically distinguish the healing involved in religious transformation from the healing worked by the therapist. However, I would question whether the theoretical dis-tinction enables him to distinguish the salvific from the therapeutic in practice. For the processes of essentialization mediated by specifically religious individuals and agencies must, for Tillich, work a psychological integration because of the unity he establishes between spirit, psyche and body in his conception of the multidimensional unity of human life.[35] Thus he will argue consistently and in a variety of ways that the process of essentialization must engage the whole of the human being or be disqualified as truly a saving process. It would seem to follow then, from his organic conception of humanity, that salvific processes cannot be disidentified from maturational processes, nor could there be a truly maturational development without a religious dimension. This means that true religious healing must work the health that the therapist seeks, and conversely that the therapist seeks a health that in one way or another has a religious dimension. The union of neurosis with faith, or worse, neurosis *as* faith, is ruled out in principle by Tillich.[36]

Due to the ontological intimacy he establishes between the dimensions of the religious and the psychological, Tillich has to admit that the therapist can be the mediator of the essential self and so of that process that religionists call salvation.[37] In an age when it is becoming increasingly apparent that depth psychology has had more to say to theology than vice versa, it is this side of Tillich's thought which needs to be emphasized and much less his rather defensive insistence that the priestly and therapeutic roles be kept apart, at least in the abstract.

This remark will serve as a transition to my third and final point. It is precisely the possibility that the therapist can be the occasion of mediating what Tillich would call the grace of the essential self that constitutes a foundational difference in the perspectives of Tillich and Jung. Tillich, as a committed Christian, had to admit this possibility but relegates it to a secondary or atypical modality in order to preserve the central point in Christian ideology, namely, that salvation is a function of grace or faith, as gift, and not of works, especially psychological work.

Tillich's Christian bias also determined his position on the related issue of his theological anthropology and its grounding in the nature of humanity as question or questioning. Here he draws a compelling picture of humanity as universally driven to ask the question of

God, but in such a manner as to receive the answer from beyond the question.[38] In doing this, Tillich is obviously concerned to preserve the priority of God in all salvational commerce with humanity, while at the same time showing humanity's need, demand and expectation of such salvation. Here the organic connectedness Tillich establishes between his theological anthropology—based on humanity's search for the essential—and his Christology—based on the Christ figure as the paradoxical realization of essence in existence—is as intimate as orthodoxy can tolerate. In establishing this organicity Tillich is to be commended.

He could go no further and still remain loyal to the Christian presupposition of the gratuity of the Christ event and of justification freely conferred by its divine author. However, in a world which since may have come to appreciate Tillich's theological anthropology more than his Christology, one might now well propose that both question and answer do in fact come from the same source, and that this source is located in the human psyche—though admittedly beyond the ego's manipulative grasp. This position would carry with it an even more intimate and organic correlation between the human quest and the agency which both prompts and answers it. Jung's psychology rests on just such an intimacy.

The specifying features of Jung's psychology derive from his personal experience of what he was later to call the collective unconscious in the period following the break with Freud.[39] Reflecting on his experience, he came to call those powers which transcend the ego and personal experience, and to which a numinous energy attaches, the archetypes. When they impact on consciousness in the form of inner drama or external hallucination, they give consciousness the impression of having been addressed by deity.[40]

Through the archetypal basis of the psyche then, Jung, like Tillich, attributes to humanity a universal religiosity which humanity cannot evade. But in the relationship between the archetypal powers of the unconscious and consciousness, Jung describes a different relation than is supposed by Tillich in his manner of relating questing humanity to answering God.

Tillich, the believer, must talk of a final revelation in Christ as *Kairos*—the fullness of time and the realization of essential humanity. Jung, on the other hand, understands the creation of religions in terms of the compensation which the collective unconscious proffers to collective consciousness, often through a prophetic or messianic individual, in its efforts to bring societal consciousness closer to a balanced wholeness. In this view, Jung gives evidence of a philosophy of history which would understand history as the process in which the unconscious seeks ever greater incarnation into consciousness, in the interests of its balance, vitality and extended empathy. With these categories Jung can appreciate the Christ event as a significant manifestation of the Self, compensating the unbridled instinctuality of the age which elicited it by providing that age with a stringent and restraining spirituality. But these same categories enable Jung to criticize the Christ image as a perhaps necessarily incomplete image of the Self, on the grounds that it cannot accommodate the reality of evil as evidenced in the split between Christ and Satan,[41] and remains uncomfortable with material creation, the body and the feminine.[42]

Jung's appreciative transcendence, and so undermining, of Christianity are most evident in his works on the Trinity and Job. In the former he pays tribute to the Trinity as an adequate symbol of the flow of psychic energy between the unconscious and the ego, but then suggests it be supplanted by a quaternity as a more adequate symbol of the differentiations and unities which the psyche naturally seeks.[43] In doing this he introduces a myth and a metaphysic ultimately forced upon him by Christianity's need for psychic completion. In Jung's compensating myth, the reality of God or of the unconscious is a seething pleroma of undifferentiated opposites, compelled to create human consciousness as the only locus where its contradictions can first be perceived and then hopefully integrated. This is the basis of his depiction of Job as a personification of that state of developing consciousness which first perceived Yaweh's narcissism, infantile swings of emotion and self-contradiction.[44]

Jung's stance in this respect makes it possible for him to pay tribute to Christianity as the religion which brings to highest historical consciousness the splits which are grounded in God and manifest fully in Christ's absolute separation from Satan. But for Jung the split consciousness at the heart of Christianity, especially in the light and dark sons (Christ and Satan) who proceed from the same Father, is to be overcome in the unity that lies beyond their mutual absolute rejection in the age of the Spirit. This age is worked by the Self as the agent first of the differentiation of the divine contradiction and then of the harmonies that arise from their reunification. But this process is one in which human historical consciousness becomes the theater for the resolution of the rifts in the ground of being.

Here Jung quite clearly departs from the Trinitarian implication that God has united the opposites in divine life prior to creation and then invites humanity, through the Spirit, to enter more fully into these pre-established harmonies, as Tillich would have it. In effect, Jung makes human consciousness the second moment or principle in divine life. Mythically, theologically and metaphysically, this means that historical consciousness has come to realize that the unresolved split in the Godhead seeks its recognition and resolution in human consciousness. Only in the process of the unconscious becoming conscious—through humanity's suffering of its contradictions toward their healing syntheses—does the work and the age of the Spirit emerge in history.

It is in this context that Jung's statement that we must seek help from God against God takes on its deepest meaning.[45] For the unconscious seems in its undifferentiated prolixity to contain a benign or redeeming agency, the latent Self, which first propels consciousness from its womb and then, with the cooperation of its child, the ego, seeks its own redemption through entrance into consciousness, using the vehicle of myth and religion collectively and the dream individually. Thus in the dialectic of the ego with the Self, it is as true to say that the Self is the generator or father of the ego as it is to say that it is the ego's son since it can become incarnate in consciousness only with the ego's cooperation.[46]

Translated into a religious idiom this means that God's need for the human is as great as the human's for God. Humanity and divinity are engaged in a process of mutual redemption, in an ontological sense, which is much more than the merely pious affirmation that humanity is somehow a cocreator with an already perfect deity.

Jung's myth implies that the unconscious, as the source of all myth, currently works to alleviate the one-sidedness of Christianity and its culture by working toward the inclusions of what it excludes. He does not seem to think that this will happen through a transforming revelation borne by an individual. Rather he implies it will happen by the less dramatic but nonetheless powerful press of the unconscious on the lives of those who suffer from the consequences of a truncated and so maiming cultural symbol system. One consequence of this view is that those who wrestle consciously with the unconscious are engaged in a sacred and eschatological task of suffering toward a wholeness currently denied, which involves God's becoming conscious in human consciousness.

Whether the more encompassing empathy that might rise from such a struggle can or will be discernibly Christian remains to be seen. Jung would fully agree with Tillich that only a symbol can replace a symbol and only a myth, a myth. He would deny that the Christian symbol could be final and press Tillich to answer a question that haunts his systematic work, especially in his reflections on the life and death of symbol systems. The question would be, "Could the Christian symbol system itself ever be legitimately surpassed?"

Is such a possibility implied in Tillich's late statement that were he to write his systematics again it would be much more from the viewpoint of the history of religions in the service of what he calls an emerging religion of the concrete spirit?[47] Though Tillich wagered that this emerging religiosity would be in some manner continuous with Pauline pneumatology,[48] does not the fact that he was forced to conjecture abouts its development imply a relativization of Christianity which at least mutes the earlier emphasis on its nature as a "final revelation"? Is this not further indicated when he emphasizes that there *may* be a central event in the history of religions which makes possible "a concrete theology that has universalistic significance?"[49] If Tillich is here referring to the Christ event, his use of the subjunctive would seem to qualify his earlier statements that identify this "central event" as the Christ event, and would deny the status of Christian faith to anyone who did not hold it as one's ultimate concern.

On the occasion of Jung's death, Tillich wrote appreciatively of the metaphysical import of Jung's "doctrine of being."[50] In this brief article Tillich holds out the hope that Jung's understanding of the archetype might dissolve the impasse between Catholic objectivity in matters dogmatic and Protestant subjectivity attaching to the experience of faith.[51] In these remarks Tillich would seem to agree with Jung that improbable mythic and dogmatic claims derive their objective historical variations from the depths of the subject. If this is the case, could Tillich then admit with Jung that the unconscious had yet to find its most adequate expression in historical religious consciousness?

Both men owe their greatness to their sense of God as dwelling in humanity's depth, and to their ability to convey this sense to a society suffering the anguish of its own superficiality. Jung would have to bow to Tillich for the precise philosophical and theological expression he gave to his experience of God as the depth and ground of his and of all being. Yet Jung from his experience of these same depths might ask Tillich to observe carefully what now proceeds from them. For Jung took his conversation with them to be an ongoing conversation with the divine. The revelation he brought back to his time was that deity continued to seek in humanity an exhaustive expression it could not find in itself, one for which it still mightily yearns.

5

Jung's Impact on Theology and Religious Studies

Jung's impact on theology and religious studies is already immense. But only currently are the more radical implications of his thought for these disciplines coming into fuller consciousness.[1]

At the heart of the impact made by Jung's psychology is its claim that it has discovered the dynamics of the psychogenesis of religious experience itself, and so has laid bare the origin of all of the religions that have both graced and bloodied human history.[2] However, Jung's identification of those archetypal energies universally endemic to the psyche which inevitably breed religious consciousness in historical humanity remains for many an ambiguous discovery. For it constitutes both a support and threat to widespread factions in the communities of religious studies and of theology, as well as to those believers they might serve beyond academe.

To understand why this is so, let us review some theological points of view together with Jung's psychological contributions.

A perennial problem of theological reflection, which remains particularly acute today, is the nature of God's presence to and activity in human life. Much of this problem revolves around the manner in which divine immanence and transcendence are related to one another. Significant Christian thinkers in the twentieth century, both Catholic and Protestant, have proposed models of God's presence to man built upon responsible affirmations of God as a power or presence immanent in life itself. Such models present divine immanence as the basis for understanding God's transcendence. These thinkers try to overcome a dualistic breach between God as immanent in creation and as transcending creation by pointing to experiences within creation that reveal a mystery beyond it.

These models establish a very intimate and ontological connection between nature, man and God, so that the divine reality is no longer understood as wholly outside of creation and imposed on creation from beyond it, but rather as experientially present to its depth and to the depth of human consciousness as the deepest stratum of both. In this way these thinkers hope to diminish the always alienating and sometimes crippling absolute discontinuity between man and God present in some modes of relating the natural and the supernatural. This they do by taking seriously the truth that God is with and in man and not only over and against him.

Maurice Blondel's measured critique of the extrinsicism of God to man present in certain methods of relating the natural to the supernatural, and his own effort to locate God in life as the immanent wellspring of human action, point to an important shift in Catholic thought to a stronger sense of God's immanence.[3] Teilhard de Chardin's efforts to depict the reality of God as a basic energy running throughout the totality of reality and working toward heightened consciousness, love and a final unity, also spring in large part from the same need to integrate more realistically the created, the human and the divine. So too Paul Tillich's understanding of God as the ground of being working in man's depths for his preservation and greater fullness of life, coupled with Tillich's critique of theologies based upon God as wholly other, bears further evidence of a keenly felt contemporary need to overcome the total split between man and God which characterized certain theologies of the not distant past and in some cases still does.

Jung's psychology has much to contribute to this quest for a model of God's presence to life capable of offsetting painful traditional dichotomies. A central contention which reappears in Jung's many religious writings is that the reality of God is discernible at the basis of life in man's unconscious. It works through its presence there to lead man into a balanced yet constantly expanding life and consciousness, in which the opposites which characterize and can destroy life become reconciled in a life-enhancing wholeness.[4]

In a certain sense Jung may be described as having at least as deep-seated and as authentic an apologetic concern as the above-mentioned theologians. He frequently expressed grave concern at the loss of power and even death of the Christian symbols for large sections of the West.[5] He was convinced that humanity would lose by this death or diminution because he thought that these symbols were grounded in humanity's collective unconscious, which he closely related to its collective wisdom and historical experience of the numinous or divine.

In Jung's view the Christian symbols grew out of the collective unconscious through a process of immediate experience combined with conscious theological elaboration. When they are alive and serve their purpose, they function to lead man to integrate his conscious with his unconscious and so to experience in a creative and controlled manner his natural rootedness in the divine.[6] With the demise of these traditional symbols (to which some still cling with a willful faith divested of the experience the symbols once conveyed) Western people have lost the "bridge" into the unconscious. As a consequence, according to Jung, Western culture is cut off from the controlled and graceful access to the divine and to its own depths once provided by the churches with their creeds or symbol systems and accompanying rites.[7]

The death of the Christian symbols does not mean that the unconscious has remained inactive. Rather the unconscious continues to work unrelated to the framework of traditional religious symbols. In this condition it invests so-called secular realities, usually ideologies ("isms"), with an ultimate and thus religious import. This process works in such a way that society is usually unaware that the loss of the traditional symbols has given rise to new ones in secular clothing.[8]

These new religions, which Jung occasionally calls social-delusional systems, are all the more insidious because they are usually not recognized as religions and so have great power to possess, deceive and brutalize man. They have produced historically as great a carnage as explicit and self-conscious religion ever did in its efforts to preserve its ultimacy, purity and claims to exclusive possession of saving truth. Thus Jung felt that Western people could be faced with the prospect of a recurrent barbarism of competing ideologies, as a result of the loss of the function of their traditional religious symbols which had served to mediate more successfully their unconscious with their conscious life.[9]

When Jung refers to society's loss of its religious symbols in the West, he is speaking explicitly of Christianity as the predominant religion of the West. However, his remarks imply that humanity is inevitably religious. Through their unconscious, people are related to a power that generates a sense of the numinous and creates myths of integration and wholeness. Beyond this implicit universalism Jung says more. While implying that the unconscious is the matrix of all human religiosity, he holds further that the major Christian symbols are peculiarly apt expressions of the unconscious, polished by centuries of conscious reflective elaboration, and so highly capable of leading the individual into that from which they have arisen.

His argument here is that the Christian symbols are grounded in humanity's collective unconscious. Thus Jung suggests that his thought could serve as the basis of a natural theology which would show how each of the major Christian symbols arises from the collective unconscious and so from its universal wisdom.[10] This suggestion does not deny that other positive religions also possess symbols that proceed from and lead into the unconscious. The difference in symbol systems among religions may be due to the different ways in which the unconscious was activated in the course of their founding revelatory events. But Jung does affirm that the symbols which have become explicit in Christianity are older and wider than Christianity itself and so are in some sense a universal human possession.[11]

The realization that Christian symbols are in some sense universal might lessen the sense of separation from, and in some cases hostility toward, other positive religions and to the world of secularity itself. Such an understanding of symbols might also serve to heal the breaches in the Christian's consciousness between the "religious" and "nonreligious" sectors of life by convincing him or her that life itself is profoundly imbued with the holy.

An examination of Jung's treatment of the major Christian symbols will reveal how he locates their origin in the unconscious and could thus speak of his psychology as providing a basis for a natural theology. It will also reveal how he endows the particular Christian symbols with a certain universality.

For Jung the Trinity, as the central symbol of Christianity, is a symbol of the dialectical relationship between the unconscious and the conscious which characterizes all of life.[12] In his view the unconscious generates consciousness, which in turn draws its living resources from the infinite creativity from which it has come, when and to the extent that it is well related to its matrix by the Spirit.[13] For Jung the purpose and underlying moral demand of life is a process he calls individuation, which he relates to one's achievement of the Self. This process involves an ever deeper interpenetration or mutual integration of the conscious and unconscious.[14] It is this process which is symbolized by historically recurrent Trinity symbolism.

In Jung's view, then, the Trinity is a symbol of the life process itself, wherein all proceeds from the Father (unconscious) as differentiated in the Son (conscious) and as related to its source through the Spirit.[15] Thus for Jung human nature as image of God is based upon the immediate participation in the dialectic of Trinitarian life cast in terms of the fruitful and inexhaustible interplay of the unconscious and ego-consciousness which, in turn, is a description of the activity of the Spirit.

In this manner of thinking, the incarnate Christ is an archetypal image of the individual at one with the source of life, the Father. Such an event meets humanity's universal expectation and demand to come into the fullest possible unity with its source. Thus Jung's Christology would depict the Christ figure as the incarnation of the fullest human possibility, namely, consciousness in unbroken unity with the divine as the basis of life.[16]

This mode of union with the unconscious also explains for Jung the meaning of sacrificial suffering in the life of Christ and, by implication, in every life.[17] Ego-consciousness relates to an infinite source, the unconscious, and as it relates more fully to and assimilates more of its source it must constantly undergo the crucifixion of dissolution as it comes into the resurrection of expanded consciousness. It is in this sense that Jung understands the meaning of the Mass as the rite of individuation in which Christ and the priest were both the sacrificer and sacrificed.[18] Not only the priest but every Christian and everyone must sacrifice and be sacrificed as ego-consciousness submits to the demands of the unconscious in the process of becoming whole and fully alive. Thus the reality of being priest and victim is universal inasmuch as everyone is caught in the dialectic between the conscious and the unconscious, and so must sacrifice and be sacrificed as the painful price of the attainment of one's truest self.

This means that for Jung the imitation of Christ is not a slavish adherence to a life model, a moral code or a set of dogmas or ritual practices extrinsic to the human and deriving from the past. Rather it is a process which constitutes the meaning of life itself, which every individual must undergo in the present in the process of becoming one's truer self. This occurs through what is often the agonizing entry into the deeper recesses of one's being, there to find a fuller life through proximity to the source of all which lies in each.[19]

Thus conceived, the experience of the reality of God—the conversion experience—occurs through a process of anamnesis, a recalling or recovery of a life-giving wholeness which was there from the outset but of which ego-consciousness frequently is unaware.[20] The reality of the divine experienced in such anamnesis arises out of life and is not imposed upon it from beyond it. Such an understanding of a latent presence of the divine power within life itself may be of great importance in overcoming the split between the natural and the supernatural. It would do this by locating grace as a divine integrating reality at the depth of the life process.[21]

In this manner does Jung ground the major symbols of Trinity, Christ, incarnation, crucifixion, sacrificial death and resurrection upon the process of the interrelation between the unconscious and consciousness.

Jung himself thought that this model of God's presence to humanity and this interpretation of the Christian symbols presupposed an understanding of God's immanence to life which would be viewed as heretical by Christian orthodoxy.[22]

This did not prevent him from relating his thought to the Christian mystical tradition and in particular to Meister Eckhart whom in turn he relates to Eastern religious thought.[23] However, he was more inclined to see his intellectual and spiritual ancestry in medieval alchemy and a more ancient gnosis than in the Christian tradition.[24] This may have been unfortunate. The twentieth-century revivification of immanental theologies may well indicate that Jung's sensitivities to the spiritual needs of moderns were sound and part of a wider movement of the religious sensibility.

Jung had profound reservations about Christian reflections on the problem of evil that reduce evil to nothing or describe it in terms of a *privatio boni*. This he felt to be an equivocation that denied the reality and power of evil. Thus his thought in places seems to take on a dualistic flavor, although an unresolved conflict between good and evil was far from his ultimate intent.[25] In relation to this problem he also felt that the Christian concept of God even as Trinitarian could not take into adequate account what he called "the missing fourth."[26]

Jung's problem of the missing fourth centers around the question of creation and its fallenness. His formulation of the question has two closely related parts. On the one hand he asks whether, if creation is wholly outside of God, it has any ultimate value. On the other hand he realizes that if creation is dialectically posited within God and God within it, then its evil quality must ultimately be attributed to God. In either case he feels that traditional Christian thought on God has been unable to account for either the necessity and worth of creation or for its fallen quality.

A similar question arises about the relationship of the feminine to the traditionally male and Trinitarian Christian God. In a highly imaginative and yet serious manner, Jung asks if there is a feminine element in the divine, and if not, then how does so male a God, and anyone who serves him, accept the feminine? This manner of putting the problem explains Jung's imaginative interpretation of the Catholic proclamation of the dogma of Mary's assumption. To Jung it meant symbolically that the feminine was finally united with and accepted by the Godhead.[27]

The underlying points in his theological critique are that the traditional understanding of a male and perfect God is incapable of showing any need in God which would give worth to creation, is incapable of taking the reality of evil seriously, and is incapable of validating the feminine whose existence it denies in the deity. It should be obvious that he is far from equating creation, evil and the feminine.

The questions Jung raises might force theologians to look once more to Platonic or neo-Platonic theological models, with which Jung may not have been familiar but which may be better suited to answer his questions. Such models portray God as a living and thus creative power who necessarily though noncompulsively shares his being beyond himself. Creation as emanation beyond the living God is seen as essentially good insofar as it continues to participate in the being of God, and even as it goes beyond him. But since creation away from God only imperfectly realizes its perfect expression within the Godhead in the Logos, it is universally fallen as it moves toward the recapturing of its essential goodness through that unqualified reunion with God to which Christian eschatological imagery has consistently pointed.

Such models have been explicitly used, for example by Bonaventure in the medieval world and by Tillich in the twentieth century. These models possess a capacity to explain the dialectic of a creation which derives its validity from the divine need for self-expression, and which retains its essential goodness even in its fallenness, better than theologies which read Genesis literally and so sever creation and especially fallen creation undialectically from God. Jung might also object to these formulations, but they do proffer the possibility of a noncontradictory affirmation at the same time of the necessity and worth of creation, of its universal fallenness, and of its ultimate healing. Hence they might better answer his questions than the theologies with which he was familiar and which failed to satisfy him.

Regarding Jung's problem with the relation of the feminine to God, an understanding of God as a living and originating force in which a creative plenitude generates the Logos—which in turn grounds created structures—might also be capable of locating a generative feminine principle within the Godhead.

In any event, the impression is inescapable that had Jung been aware of the movement toward immanental approaches to God by Christian thinkers in the twentieth century, he would have been less ready to designate himself a heretic. Part of the problem lies with Christian theological development which in recent centuries seems to have lost a significant section of itself, namely the neo-Platonic tradition which derives from Augustine and others. Such a tradition possesses a much more lively sense of the presence of the God within and so has greater resources for a theological anthropology based upon humanity's natural ontological and epistemological participation in the divine. Put briefly, thinkers such as Jung may have falsely judged themselves unorthodox because orthodoxy itself lost half of itself when it lost its sense of God as immanent.

Among moderns, Paul Tillich in particular called for a revival of an Augustinian anthropology to overcome the division which had pitted God and man against each other as opposites. This division also lay at the heart of the split between faith and reason and theology and the other sectors of culture and thought.[28] In Tillich's view, a return to a concept of divine immanence which would underlie all of reality and give to it a sense of unity and meaning would heal these breaches at the theological level. Jung fully experienced these breaches himself and saw their disastrous effects in the psychic and religious lives of his patients and clients.

Both Tillich and Jung seem to agree in identifying an important factor in humanity's present spiritual distress—the absence of a sense of creation and life naturally imbued with the presence of God and so with meaning. It would be ironic and tragic if certain theologies have contributed to this absence. By pointing to it and to the suffering that follows from it, Tillich and Jung have also pointed to its possible alleviation, insofar as it can be alleviated by thought alone.

*

What, then, are the "radical implications" of Jung's thought, alluded to at the beginning of this chapter? And why does Jung's claim to have discovered the psychogenesis of religious experience in the unconscious constitute both a support and a threat to theology and religious studies?

Jung's discovery is profoundly supportive of religious studies because it shows that humanity, as long as it is endowed with its current psychic constitution, must give expression to its religious impulse. With the discrediting and political dispossession of institutional religion in the Enlightenment and its wake, Jung feared that collective religious expression in the twentieth century had taken on

political rather than indentifiably religious forms. Thus, as mentioned above, the energies previously channeled into religious commitment had been transformed into the various political "isms" with
which the twentieth century has been so abundantly blessed and
cursed.[30] Despite his profound reserve regarding the transformation
which moved the religious energies of the psyche from specifically
religious to political expression, Jung nevertheless argues consistently that humanity cannot rid itself of its religiosity or of its need
for a religious component, however disguised. Typically, this manifests in the *participation mystique* and in the *representations collec-
tives* which paradoxically provide the cohesive myths which make
societies possible, even as they lower the consciousness of their
national or tribal constituencies in doing so.

On this basis the religionist is given profound assurance that the
study of religion is the study of the deepest level of the human
reality, namely, of the depths of the psyche from whence deity
addresses humanity in a conversation that can never end. But precisely because the conversation continues indefinitely, Jung's
psychology becomes the basis for a possible radical reinterpretation
of the task of both the religionist and the theologian.

In the face of the full challenge of Jung's psychology, their task
might well assume the stature of a reflection on the ongoing conversation between deity and humanity under the rubric of how better
to conduct this dialogue in the birthing of a safer God, in a myth
with a wider empathy, and, as such, possessed of a greater survival
value than those divisive myths currently extant and ruling. As will
be seen, this task would be greatly facilitated should the practitioner
of these disciplines have individual, immediate and experiential
access to those energies in his or her psyche from which religion
universally arises.

However, many of those who are beginning to realize the wider
implications of Jung's understanding of the psychogenesis of religion rightly see it to be a mixed blessing. They are not wrong in
looking upon it as a serious threat to claims of any faith to have a
so-called "final revelation" of an exclusive or even privileged
nature. For such a mind set Jung's understanding remains a threat
because, while it can appreciate all mythical-religious expressions,
it cannot attribute an unqualified finality to any.

On the contrary, the spirit of Jung's thought suggests that humanity's dialogue with deity remains in a preliminary stage. It would view suggestions that this dialogue had reached full maturation in one or other of its discrete historical expressions as somehow juvenile. As such Jung's psychology works an appreciative undermining of all current historical concretions of the religion-making propensities of the psyche, at least in their claim to an exhaustive finality. Indeed, his psychology, read organically, implies that all such expressions, valuable in themselves, seek now their own transcendence and so transformation—if not actual negation—toward a consciousness of wider embrace and greater empathy, both prompted and demanded by the natural movement or *telos* of the psyche itself.

Three themes in Jung's understanding of the psyche's religious and God-making propensities are at the basis of the fear of those who distrust his insight in these matters, and at the basis of the hope of those attracted by it. These are the themes of interiorization, relativization and universalization. Let us consider each one separately, though they admittedly intersect in the organic nature of his psychology.

Interiorization implies that the making of religion, with its attendant myths, rites, dogmas and moralities, is a psychic process which cannot accomodate any agency working on the psyche from beyond it. Thus for Jung efforts to "get God out of the psyche," in the interests of preserving some kind of divine transcendence in principle unrelated to the human, are doomed to failure. On this issue Jung is quite clear in the epistemological consequences of his psychology. Only that can be known which is known through the psyche.[31] If the experience of deity is not mediated through the native functioning of the psyche as both the possibility and necessity of humanity's experience of divinity, it could not be mediated at all. God would remain, in principle, beyond human experience and so be of no significance to humanity.

Moreover, Jung might well look askance at the motives of those interested in "getting God out of the psyche." For Jung, success in this dubious enterprise would result in variations of depression or rage. These are the inevitable consequences of being deprived, or depriving oneself, of those libidinal energies which fund life's efforts and which, in certain configurations of intensity, Jung identifies with the experience of God and of grace.[32]

Thus relating Jung's understanding of the creation of religion to processes of psychic interiority hostile to efforts to "get God out of the psyche" does serve to illuminate a major implication of what is involved in interiorization. For Jung's psychology establishes so intimate a link between human consciousness and the archetypal energies that convince it of deity's reality that a conception of God as "wholly other" than humanity, is, for Jung, wholly inconceivable.[33]

In Jung's mind such a conception of God remains one of the major pathologizing features of the Western religious tradition. It would remove from the fabric of life itself the psychic energies which fund life, or it would project the source of these energies beyond life into transcendent dieties whose ability to lend energy to life is greatly impaired by the projection itself. This removal of the victim of belief from life's energies is further worsened when the believer is then asked in the name of faith to relate to such deity through myth, dogma and creeds which for modern consciousness are all too often what Jung calls "preposterous nonsense."[34]

But Jung's concept of interiorization does more than convict orthodox conceptions of divine transcendence of pathologizing their victims by removing God as the source of life from life itself. His own conception of interiorization, especially as expressed in his work on Job[35] and on the symbol of the Trinity,[36] moves from a Trinitarian to a quaternitarian understanding of deity as present to humanity. In this move Jung introduces major features of the myth which envigorates his own psychology. It is a myth which bears an appreciative transcendence of the Jewish-Christian myth, as well as other myths, founded on a deity conceived to exist in potential discontinuity from humanity and human consciousness.

In the move to a quaternitarian model Jung implies that deity in itself is no doubt intensely creative, but is driven to create out of its need to become aware in created human consciousness of its own antinomy or self-contradiction. This clearly implies that human consciousness, infinitely weaker than its divine matrix, is yet gifted with that power of discretion which can perceive in the Godhead the contradiction the Godhead could neither perceive nor resolve in itself.[37] Only then, through the cooperation of the human, can deity move to resolve the split in the ground of its being, not in the transcendent remove of a self-sufficient Trinity but in the processes of human historical consciousness.

Thus the radical immanence of Jung's conception of deity implies that human consciousness and creation as a whole is no arbitrary superaddition to deity's pre-existent and splendid isolation. Rather Jung would have it that human consciousness proceeds from the Godhead much as do those processions in the more traditional understanding of the Trinity, but with the added dignity and burden that in human consciousness alone can deity seek the resolution of the contradiction it could not find in itself.

With this shift in perspective Jung lays to rest all theological pretensions to a Trinitarian God eternally perfectly differentiated in its own life process, and moving to create beyond itself in a moment somehow consequent to and independent of its own differentiation. To get at the radical shift in paradigm this move implies it could be said that Jung would understand human consciousness itself as the second principle in the processions of the Godhead. So understood, human consciousness would be the Logos, but a Logos which painfully reflects the split in its origin and, paradoxically, with the help of that origin, seeks to unify its opposites in the fourth. In this paradigm the age of the Spirit would point to that stage of human consciousness which had first perceived and then resolved the primordial contradiction in its source, at the insistence and with the help of that source itself.

Thus in Jung's myth it becomes as true to say that humanity is involved in the redemption of God as to say that God is engaged in the redemption of humanity. The new and horrifying moral imperative attached to this position is humanity's charge, first to discern the unresolved contradiction in deity, and then to embrace the suffering burden of becoming the vehicle or container in which this contradiction can be resolved. Its resolution then becomes at once the challenge at the heart of the suffering in each individual life, the substance of history, and the basis of the philosophy of history latent in Jung's psychology.

Such are some of the implications for the phenomenon of religion and its study of what I have called interiorization as it works in Jung's psychology. Let us now pass to the second theme of discussion, that of relativization.

Jung understands the psyche to be enlivened by a dialectic in which an infinite pole, the unconscious, seeks its expression in the finitude of consciousness.[38] In another aspect of his thought related to this dialectic, he suggests that the archetypes may be of an inexhaustible fecundity as they express themselves in human consciousness. This too would imply that they need many variant concretions to even approximate what they want to express in consciousness. Both points work toward a relativization of all expressions of the unconscious. This is particularly true of its major expressions, which are inevitably mythical-religious and which provide humanity with the needed belief systems on which to found its personal convictions and social organization.

The greater challenge of Jung's thought in this area centers on the question of whether the unconscious can ever exhaustively express itself in consciousness. The eschatological imagery of many religious traditions would seem to imply that it can and that this is the direction in which world history moves. Such, for instance, would be the import of the image of the New Jerusalem in which God will be "all in all." Given the historical performances of the religions which bear such imagery when they try to realize it in—or, more tragically, impose it upon—historical society, it may be safer to hold the consciousness to which eschatological imagery points as a distant possibility. In holding eschatological hope at bay, and thus bargaining for time in the face of its too often apocalyptic urgencies, humanity both collectively and individually could work more responsibly toward the birthing of a safer myth through conscious dialogue with the unconscious.

From the individual's immediate experience of those energies that give rise to religion universally, a growing and freeing appreciation of religious experience might well arise. This appreciation of religion, through the experience of its basis in the Self, would both convince consciousness of its positive energies as well as relativize specific religious expression and commitments. Such experience appears foundational to Jung's psychology and is the basis of the methodology and hermeneutic his thought contains. Such a hermeneutic would be well aware that any religious revelation is made more intelligible through comparison with its historical variants. Where there were no variants one could assume one was dealing with the freakish and so with that which held little value for the human condition. For example, one would best understand the Christian myth by looking for its extra-Christian variants—in such candidates as the myths and rites of Osiris or Dionysus, in the host of counterclaims to be in possession of the Logos incarnate in whatever form, or in the modern variants of the *anthropos* myth in such secular religions as Marxism.

Thus the encompassing perspective which emerges from a Jungian conception of relativization is the view that the efforts of the unconscious to give itself full expression in human historical consciousness are still in progress, and that any of its major expressions to date must be understood through a reflection on their variants. This reflection would at once illuminate what it is that seeks expression in these variants, while persuading the mind that no variant to date exhausts the wealth of what seeks expression in it. Again, claims to exhaustive possession of a saving truth are negated toward collective safety, even as an openness to going beyond our current religious consciousness is made possible and necessary.

This brings us to our last theme, the Jungian conception of universalization. If interiorization means that all religions originate from an intrapsychic dynamic, and if relativization means that no myth exhausts the archetypal energies that seek expression in it, universalization refers to the fact that all enduring myths have universal significance as expressions of the psyche's deepest movement. Needless to say, this is true not only of the so-called living religions but also of those called dead. Many an analyst has witnessed the truth of so-called dead religions, with modern variants of their gods and goddesses alive and well in the contemporary psyche.

Indeed one wonders what refusal of wealth prompted the psyche so widely to reduce the many gods to one.

The best example of the implications of universalization in Jung's writings are in those passages in which he effectively refutes the efforts of orthodox Christianity to turn the truth of Christ, understood as the unity of the human and divine in an isolated individual, into a unique event. Jung states explicitly that the unconscious could never countenance the reduction of the unity of the divine and the human to one historical individual.[39] By this he means that the unity of the divine and the human is a universal human possibility, one whose realization in each life is demanded by the dynamics of the psyche in the natural process of human maturation. As such, incarnation becomes for Jung a major paradigm for processes of individuation, understood as the progressive unification of conscious and unconscious.[40]

There is a sense in Jung's thought in which the truth of Christ, for example, is a universal truth, but not one which is of any consolation to that religious sensitivity which would claim uniqueness or finality for it, and hold it to have a universal validity for all times and cultures. For, when the universal truth of Christ is related to the implications of Jung's conception of relativization, this truth becomes but one concretion of the power of the Self. This is not to deny its current importance since, argues Jung with considerable justification, it continues to provide our society with its culture hero.[41] Jung makes this point explicitly when he states that Christ is an image of the Self, not the Self an image of Christ.[42]

In this example taken from the Christian myth, one sees clearly how the processes of interiorization, relativization and universalization conspire to undermine religious claims to uniqueness and finality, while appreciating the power of the archetypal motifs these religions embody.

One sees also how these processes, intrinsic to the dynamic of the unconscious as it generates religious experience, when engaged with consciously by individual and ultimately by society could contribute to a more user-friendly myth as the basis of a more tolerant social consciousness. This would be the case because immediate experience of the unconscious would acquaint the individual with his or her personal myth as the basis of relating to collective myths. This would free the individual from the tyranny of a myth not one's own and in so doing, Jung would contend, make a most valuable contribution to a safer social climate by modifying collective absolutes in favor of individual spiritual needs.

The import of these remarks leads to the following conclusions about Jung's impact on the disciplines of theology and religious studies. There is a discernible norm in a Jungian hermeneutic which can be brought to bear on the field of religious studies. It would divide approaches to the field into those aware of the origin of religious consciousness and its expressions in the unconscious, and those which are unaware of the origin of the content of their discipline. The latter approach could then justly be designated as unconscious in a negative sense, because such an approach remains oblivious to the origin and so to the nature of religion itself.[43]

In the neighboring field of theology, this normative aspect of Jung's hermeneutic could lead to a new understanding of fundamentalist thought. Fundamentalism would be seen as that form of unconsciousness which is induced in the mind of the believer grasped and imprisoned by the archetypal power of the cherished myth. That theology could then be identified as fundamentalist in which the believing mind, reflecting on its myth in the doing of theology, remained unaware of the origin in the unconscious of both the myth itself and of the faith in the myth which prompts theological reflection upon it.

Thus, possibly the most significant implication of Jung's thought for theology and religious studies is his challenge and invitation to the practitioner to experience individually and immediately the energies that birth the material with which he or she deals. In doing so, Jung's approach could cultivate a transformation in the consciousness of its practitioners, which in turn could enable these disciplines to become significant contributors to the currently developing family of sciences of human survival.

6

Of Human Faiths and Kidney Stones

Sustained reflection on Jung's treatment of humanity's religion-making propensities is at once disturbing and provocative and yet finally bracing. It is all these things because of the way Jung so explicitly grounds religious consciousness in the life of the psyche itself and so makes religion and all that attends it an historical necessity. But even as he does this he points to religion's ambivalent historical performance and suggests that its many modern faces may destroy the very humanity which is fated to create it.

This dark paradox at the heart of Jung's thought on religion might well sustain an extended analogy between the generation and performance of religious consciousness and communities in history, and the growth of kidney stones in the body. The medical profession assures us that there is little point in surgically removing these stones, since they tend to replace themselves at the point in the living organ where they have been generated and from which they are removed. An extensive reading of Jung's position on the psychogenesis of religious consciousness reveals that, though myths and religions may replace one another and gods and goddesses may come and go, no society or individual is without them. More to the point, attempts to remove them surgically—as reason attempted to do in and since the Enlightenment—have proved to date to be dismal failures.

Jung argues, with considerable backing from history, that where the gods and goddesses were discredited in their identifiably religious form, they returned as political "isms" with the same insatiable thirst for human life previously shown in their more easily recognizable religious faces. Thus at the heart of Jung's critique of political faiths, even in a so-called secular world, is his suggestion that they live from the same archetypal energies that previously funded religious faith and so can render their adherents equally unconscious.

A more crucial point in the analogy between stones in the kidneys and religions in history is the fact that stones in sufficient numbers can force the removal and so death of the organ that generates them. As members of a commonly held humanity, we are faced today with the problem that we may be collectively terminated by the conflict between religious convictions and the communities these convictions generate, much as the ill-fated kidney dies from its own concretions.

The identification of a deeper hope in Jung's thought on religion can only be honest if it faces squarely the dilemma posed by it. The dilemma is this: because of the nature and dynamics of the psyche, humanity cannot live without its religious myths and faiths, but because of the conflicts between communities possessed by these myths humanity may face a brief future.

Aware of the genocidal possibility latent in all collective forms of archetypal possession, Jung warned of "those impersonal forces which make you an unconscious instrument of the wholesale murderer in man."[1] This theme of the murderer possessed by faith runs as a dark current throughout Jung's thought on religion and its modern political equivalents. He compares modern political faiths to the medieval epidemics of bubonic plague, pointing out that the former have a higher body count than the latter and are no less a plague because they originate in the human psyche and not in a virus. About such epidemics of faith a typical passage by Jung reads:

> The fascination which is almost invariably connected with ideas of this sort produces a fanatical obsession, with the result that all dissenters, no matter how well meaning or reasonable they are, get burnt alive or have their heads cut off or are disposed of in masses by the more modern machine-gun.[2]

Nor does Jung relate such faith to the past, for he immediately goes on in the passage just cited to speak of the present and future in these words: "We cannot even console ourselves with the thought that such things belong to the remote past. Unfortunately they seem to belong not only to the present, but, quite particularly, to the future."[3]

Jung's reference to the future makes his problem with religion our problem, one which drives quickly to the question, "Can we lose our divisive faiths in time to save our collective humanity? And if so, how?" For Jung these questions are different from the similar sounding questions posed by the Enlightenment in the name of a reason confident of its ability to banish the gods and goddesses from the realm of the human or to reduce them to their common denominator in humanity's interest. Jung would argue that this is not possible, as witness the work of the political deities in whose name and with whose power the slaughter continues on this side of the Age of Reason.

It follows, then, that an organic reading of Jung would deny the possibility of a lived atheism, would see it rather as a form of self-deception and a dangerous intellectual luxury that humanity on the brink of a final holy war can no longer entertain. The question is not whether there is to be a myth or not. On this question we have no choice. The question is whether and how we can now contribute to the formation of a myth bearing a religious consciousness, one whose reigning power would serve rather than consume the humanity through whom it is given birth. Indeed, Jung's thought suggests that the birthing into consciousness of such a myth is humanity's most urgent current need and task. Such a myth would have to bear a more encompassing empathy, one capable of countering our current compulsion to pit our communal selves against each other in the name of competing revelations whose "Good News" may be quickly turning terminal.

If Jung's thought is not to contribute to the death of our hope in the future with its stern reminders of how our faiths have functioned in the past, can we find in it the seeds of a counter, complementary, or even a possibly supplanting myth, one whose emerging power might be currently experienced and whose energies would make the future first possible and then richer?

If there is such a basis for hope in Jung's understanding of the psyche, I would look for it in Jung's eschatology, that side of his experience of the psyche which relates the present to the future in terms of the deeper unifying and so healing energies always at work in individual and society. Our ability to cultivate these energies by bringing them to conscious symbolic expression may be our ultimate resource in shaping a usable and enjoyable future.

Though Jung uses the term "eschatology" only seven times in his *Collected Works,* he reveals the centrality and urgency of his concern with how the present might move to the future in one of his major and later letters to Father Victor White. In this letter of December 1953, in a perhaps unguarded moment, Jung comes very close to presenting himself and his vision as a modern reincarnation of Joachim di Fiore, the twelfth-century monk who proclaimed the nearness of the age of the Spirit, when humanity and divinity would thoroughly pervade each other and God would be all in all. Jung describes himself as a modern Joachim in these words:

> Thus I am approaching the end of the Christian aeon and I am to take up Gioacchino's anticipation and Christ's prediction of the coming of the Paraclete. This archetypal drama is at the same time exquisitely psychological and historical. We are actually living in the time of the splitting of the world and of the invalidation of Christ.[4]

But in the paragraph immediately following these remarks, Jung introduces the paradox that lies at the heart of his psychology as it touches religion and its future. In this passage I would take him to say that the same Spirit which has sponsored the Christian dispensation is the Spirit which currently invalidates it toward the future when he writes:

> But an anticipation of a faraway future is no way out of the actual situation. It is a mere *consolamentum* for those despairing at the atrocious possibilities of the present time. Christ is still the valid symbol. Only God himself can "invalidate" him through the Paraclete.[5]

These passages seem to lead Jung into a flat contradiction. On the one hand he argues that the symbol of Christ is still valid and on the other that it is to be invalidated by the same Spirit which authored it. What lies behind this apparent contradiction is the ground theme and mystery at the heart of Jung's metapsychology. This theme would argue that the Spirit of the unconscious, the Self, constellates opposites in history in order to unite them in a higher, richer and more inclusive consciousness. Thus the Holy Spirit must work the absolute contradiction between, for instance, the opposites of good and evil, Christ and Satan, as the first movement toward their reunion at a higher level in a seemingly impossible embrace.

I say "seemingly impossible," for we still are at a total loss to even imagine how the figures of Christ and Satan could come to a realization of their common descent from the one Father, and, in recognizing their fraternity, move to resolve their conflict. From Jung's perspective, if this conflict were to be eternalized it would confirm the mutual failure of the divine and human to move beyond myths of ultimate division and mutual exclusion.

Throughout his work Jung establishes a complex dialectic on the issue of Christianity's transcending the absolute contradictions at the heart of its myth, best exemplified in the split between Christ and Satan. On the one hand he thought it a social tragedy if Christianity were to be prematurely dismissed—largely because of its self-destructive literalism and loss of the symbolic sense—before the relative truth of the absolute contradiction in the Godhead, reflected in the opposition between Christ and Satan, were to be understood and lived through. It is evident from his work on Job that he gave to the Christian myth its highest value for making as explicit as possible the archetypal antinomy alive in the unconscious and so dramatically expressed in the interplay between Christ and Satan. Thus when the Christ figure says, "Get thee behind me, Satan," no doubt lingers about the absolute incompatibility of the two.

Yet Jung remained equally painfully aware that the much needed conscious differentiation of the absolute opposition between Christ and Satan could not be final. The unconscious, having worked the opposition with the help of the Christian myth, now gropes for a myth which would work the needed reunion. Such a myth would gratefully appreciate its Christian precedent without which it could not become a sought-for possibility and necessity. But in seeking to unify in consciousness the antinomy at the heart of the Christian myth, its appreciation might well also become an appreciative transcendence undermining the Christian myth. In my opinion Jung's own psychology implies such an appreciative transcendence of Christianity, and is itself one of the more significant bearers of the new myth of reintegration.

Let me attempt to capture the paradigm shift involved in Jung's myth by retelling it in a religious idiom of my own formulation. It would be made up of two foundational themes in Jung's psychology, themselves in some tension. The first is the unresolved contradiction in the unconscious itself. The second is its unremitting drive first to differentiate and then to resolve its contradictions in consciousness.

Religiously, the first theme might be put this way: In the beginning God had a nervous breakdown. The event is lost in the primordial past and so its cause cannot be fully recovered. Certain psychological and theological circles may be moving toward the consensus that its cause lay in the realization by the Godhead that it simply could not hold together the wealth of the conflicting opposites which made up its seething but profoundly unconscious life. Out of this moral crisis, which follows the failure of any life process to find its center and to give adequate expression to its truth, the creation of human consciousness was made necessary as the only place where the divine problem could be solved. Thus out of the original breakdown human consciousness slowly emerged and, in the minds of a few like Job and certainly in the mind of Jung interpreting Job, humanity became aware of its destiny to redeem its divine origin in history and in so doing to redeem itself.

But this awareness dawned slowly, born from the blood bath of faiths in conflict in history. The conflict was itself due to the immensity and diversity of the energies within the Godhead whose uncentered prolixity provoked the initial creative disintegration, the collapse that resulted in God's problems becoming ours. At the heart of the problem was the seemingly insuperable difficulty that any significant component of the divine psyche, supernatural complexes so to speak, had sufficient energy to be taken by clusters of humans possessed by them as the totality. When the chosen became deeply possessed by these partialities they re-enacted in history the divine failure that gave rise to it. In the name of a revealed partiality, they could not tolerate a wider totality or counterpartialities and so slaughtered all who would not accept their revealed truncation.

With time human consciousness became more aware of its victimization by its origin. It saw more clearly the flaw in the foundation, the unresolved split in the ground of being. Contentions implicit in Trinitarian theology that the Creator somehow had it together before drawing land out of water, consciousness out of its precedent, became less credible as a sense of divine unconsciousness and so divine psychic and moral irresponsibility became more pervasive.

In the trials of Job, Jung saw an early expression of humanity's dawning awareness of the contradictions in its Creator with the horrible responsibility attendant on such realization.[6] Only humanity can be the place of the redemption of the divine, by consciously suffering its contradictions in a process which brings together in human life what divinity could not bring together in its own. With this realization die all conceptions of a God or human in whom there is no darkness. Out of this death rises the stark assurance that moral responsibility henceforth entails grappling with the shadow of God in the process of its historical redemption. Nowhere is the human recognition of the unresolved ambivalence in deity and the human moral responsibility attached to this recognition more succinctly put than when Jung writes of God:

> He fills us with evil as well as with good, otherwise he would not need to be feared; and because he wants to become man, the uniting of his antinomy must take place in man. This involves man in a new responsibility.[7]

Jung's "Answer to Job" is a lengthy, almost systematic, reflection, at times approaching poetry, on the dialectic involved in the discussion between the unconscious and the ego, between divinity and humanity, as they seek their mutual redemption through their mutual interpenetration. Here Jung works a masterful synthesis between the psychological, the eschatological and the historical. His thrust is that the unconscious seeks the redemptive resolution of its opposites in human consciousness. This resolution comes only through patterns of repeated suffering. The death of the old and conflicted consciousness is the price of the union of the divine opposites in resurrected consciousness, with the extended embrace and empathy attaching to resurrection thus understood.

For Jung, then, the answer to Job and the meaning of the incarnation and death of Christ are one. These archetypal events point to the process of God becoming conscious in human consciousness, in that mutual agony in which the divine contradiction is perceived and resolved in humanity in repeated rhythms of death and resurrection. This process is psychological because its theater is the human psyche and yet, because it is the goal of the one psychic process at work in history, is also profoundly historical and eschatological. All of this is summed up in a passage which captures in less than a paragraph Jung's synthesis of the psychological, the religious and the historical. He writes:

> There is no evidence that Christ ever wondered about himself, or that he ever confronted himself. To this rule there is only one significant exception—the despairing cry from the Cross; "My God, my God, why hast thou forsaken me?" Here his human nature attains divinity; at that moment God experiences what it means to be a mortal man and drinks to the dregs what he made his faithful servant Job suffer. Here is given the answer to Job, and, clearly, this supreme moment is as divine as it is human, as "eschatological" as it is "psychological."[8]

Later in "Answer to Job" Jung puts the same point more succinctly and in a manner that makes more evident the connection between the psychic and religious, as well as the underlying historical dimensions involved: "The unconscious wants to flow into consciousness in order to reach the light, but at the same time it continually thwarts itself, because it would rather remain unconscious. That is to say, God wants to become man, but not quite."[9]

This power, which both flees from and yet seeks consciousness in history, Jung sometimes describes as the matrix or mother of historical consciousness and so gives it the maternal and feminine meaning of the Great Goddess from whom all lesser gods and goddesses descend. At times he describes this divinity in more masculine terms as the *deus absconditus*, the hidden God, whose energies bred of self-contradiction cry out for historical resolution in human consciousness.[10]

By whatever name he calls her, Jung, keenly aware of the divine reticence to become fully incarnate and so conscious, nevertheless seems finally to wager that the divine mother of consciousness pushes with all her might to become fully conscious in history.

Where her processes become petrified or stereotyped, she uses her full archetypal powers against the logjam, whether political or religious, in the creation of a newer and safer, because more embracing, myth. Just as Paul Tillich would argue that only a myth replaces a myth and a symbol a symbol, so might Jung argue that only an archetype can dissolve a stereotype.

If humanity's religious quest has currently hardened into the stereotyped one-and-only Gods glaring at each other through the eyes of their devotees in armed camps, one would look then to see where the newer and safer myth may be becoming visible in today's world. Where is God being redeemed in the form of a higher, more inclusive consciousness beyond the congealed communities of hate who may like kidney stones end the life of the organ that bred them?

Let us look for the answer to this question first in the collective and then in the individual. From the viewpoint of collective religious or political leadership, Jung's myth and its eschatology must appear at least abrasive and possibly heretical. Can either religious or political leaders entrusted with the care and promulgation of their respective competitive myths respond to the breadth of Jung's? Can they admit that their ultimates, their so-called final revelations, have led so unerringly to final solutions? Are they truly capable of sponsoring a saving doubt in the interests of a myth of survival? Could, for instance a new devotion be struck to the Holy Mother of Saving Doubt? Those who worship her might be the harbingers of a meaningful undermining of the certitudes that currently divide and so often kill. Her devotees could at the same time be confident that out of the pain of the loss of the comforting but lethal certitudes which the Mother of Saving Doubt would dissolve, a more humane myth and faith might arise.

But are our leaders up to the appreciative transcendence of their current eternal but partial truths in the name of a greater wholeness than they currently can mediate? Or are the sons and daughters of Thomas Jefferson and John Wayne to continue to stare down their gun-sights at the spiritual descendents of Hegel and Marx, while Christians, mercifully deprived of their armies—at least in the West—opt between "the free world" or "liberation theology"? But none seek liberation from theology as that form of unconsciousness which gives divine warrant to our absolutes written in stone and, if not dissolved, are destined to turn us into it.

It would appear that significant collective alleviation of the current danger of contending monomyths should not be looked on with an easy optimism. It would mean the cultivation of a consciousness in religious and political leadership, and in those led, which would be acutely aware that claims to absolute or even highly privileged possession of a saving religious or political truth are the ultimate sin against the human spirit, the ultimate form of social irresponsibility, and the deepest current threat to our collective survival. It would mean the widespread cultivation of a consciousness which would respond to claims of infallibility or to a decisive revelation in one or other sacred event and its literal record, as proceeding from a profoundly antihuman impulse whose historical performance must now be reversed in the name of the continuity of the life these traditions claim to serve but so often destroy.

This side of Jung's myth would challenge mainstream myths and their theological interpreters to overcome the ruptures and peculiar insensitivities that continue to inform both myth and interpretation. How transcendent, how wholly other, can God remain when God is experienced as the plea and demand by the deeper psyche that its divisions be brought together in consciousness in the healing of life? How can a distinction between the natural and the supernatural remain, when individual and society become widely aware that it is as natural to deal with the supernatural as it is to face the conflictual energies of the psyche as the background of our consciousness? What happens to doctrines of the corruption of humanity when the perception spreads that simply to be human means inevitably to be addressed by the pressure of divinity seeking its redemption in the process of humanity's becoming whole?

Particularly in the current crucial area of a militant apocalypticism—the idea that one or other God or messianic figure will return in power to justify a discrete but now harassed remnant—does Jung's myth offer an appreciative undermining of immense social value. He convicts apocalyptic consciousness in any of its various stripes of an infantile and unqualified certitude that would rather flee or end the world than deal with the tensions and contradictions

involved in life in the world. The distaste for life and its vicis-
situdes, and the religiously induced hostility toward the opponent
or contradictor latent in all such literature, must come to be seen
for the expressions of hatred that they are. They must be trans-
cended in the name and with the assistance of a more encompassing
empathy. Jung expressed his own rejection of the hopeless one-
sidedness of even the Christian apocalyptic images of the New
Jerusalem and the marriage of the Lamb in these words:

> No doubt this is meant as a final solution of the terrible conflict of
> existence. The solution, however, as here presented, does not consist
> in the reconciliation of the opposites, but in their final severance,
> by which means those whose destiny it is to be saved can save
> themselves by identifying with the bright pneumatic side of God.[11]

The myth which would replace such pathologizing one-sidedness
and eternal splitting of humanity and deity would involve what Jung
calls the relativization of God. It would be more capable of seeing
an authentic divine presence in a plethora of revelations. It would
realize that a God struggling to give balance and definition to divine
life in history would probably need many such revelations as such
a God moved toward divine maturity through increasing human
maturity. Such consciousness would also bring with it a redeeming
embarrassment at being a member of "the chosen," if such were the
case, as the first step in grappling with the tragedy, personal and
social, which such status implies.

Yet, after two millenia of "the truth which sets free," we should
not expect the captains of our truth-bearing communities to endorse
too readily the doubt that may set even freer. If we are candid, such
prophets of militant doubt have few historic precedents and the note
sounded too often by contemporary prophets seems to lack the gra-
cious tentativeness which Jung expresses when he writes, "I for my
part prefer the precious gift of doubt, for the reason that it does not
violate the virginity of things beyond our ken."[12]

If the carriers of collective consciousness seem still largely comfortable with the kind of faiths that have sustained them in the past
but now may be growing terminal, can we look to individual consciousness to bear the newer myth? Indeed, I suspect that Jung's

preference lies in this direction. Throughout his work Jung returns in variations to the central theme that only the individual is the bearer of consciousness. In many places he insists that if humanity is to extract itself from the epidemics of faith that have ravaged its history and shaken its hope, including all forms of the "isms" that empower modern genocide,[13] it can only do so through a process of individuals freeing themselves from the unconsciousness that commits them through faith, as freedom's enemy, to communities of conflict.

The question then arises why individuals might better bear the doubt that sets free and its extended empathies when institutions cannot. The answer which Jung might well propose, one which is compatible with many streams in religious studies and history, is that newer and freer myths are often born into consciousness through those who suffer most under the old. This insight might provide both religious and political communities with the basis of a self-critical hermeneutic, a hermeneutic of the suffering—understood as those who suffer under these institutions and their questionable dispensation of grace. The sheep shorn by the shepherd on the way to becoming mutton is in a peculiarly apt position to question seriously the waters and grasslands into which she or he is being allegedly led.

But, again, why will individual suffering consciously borne be more likely to yield the pearl of great price, the Philosopher's Stone or the inner diamond? Why will it not produce simply another kidney stone? This question would arise with all the more urgency if the Godhead whose presence is most readily felt in the heart of human suffering has created human consciousness to heal a split it could not heal in its own life. What help can ever be expected from such a God?

This brings us in conclusion to the second foundational theme that runs through Jung's myth. It would go this way. Though God was driven to create human consciousness in that breakdown following the divine realization that the primordial contradiction at the heart of the divine character could only be solved in history and not in heaven, yet like many a deeply disturbed human life, some solid core remained. In that surviving core Jung locates the Self of both every individual and of the cosmological reality itself. The latter reality Jung sometimes calls the *anima mundi,* the soul of the world. The process he calls individuation is one in which the soul of the individual, through many a death and resurrection, comes increasingly to live out of its experiential inherence in the life of the world's soul.

Where this wedding of the individual to the soul of the world occurs, the individual is graced with the experience of his or her wholeness and with a not unexpected empathy for the totality since, within the soul, the individual approximates unity with the source of the totality. Such experience Jung equates with the experience of grace and of God. He makes it the direction or *telos* toward which every life and life universal move. As such it is the substance of his psychology, the basis of his philosophy of history and of his eschatology, and, finally, the ground of the profound hope his psychology proffers to humanity.

Into this world of personal wholeness and universal connectedness one enters alone through the portals of one's interiority, and not infrequently after the repeated pain of looking for it in vain beyond oneself. It is because of the constant presence of this possibility in the depths of the soul that Jung looks to the individual first to discover it there, and then, to the extent possible, to share it with the collective toward the extension of its sympathies.

In a final cautionary note I would add that the addictive power, the compelling charm, of such experienced wholeness is probably the basis of all eschatological hope and its varied expressions in sacred literatures. As such it also bears that dark side of hope which metastisizes so often, so easily and so violently into our disparate and dispersive myths, each with their own exclusive and privileged version of the final coming together. When these myths rape the hope that creates them by locating the place or person of their final fulfillment within geographical boundaries—whether, for instance, of Jerusalem, Rome, Mecca, Washington or Moscow—they produce the carnage that lust for the Kingdom of God seems always to produce when taken literally.

Thus the divine compulsion to heal its initial wound in human life and history must come to be seen by the humanity through whom it works as both our ultimate resource and threat. To date this divine compulsion in history seems to have produced addict and murderer with the same abundant disdain as it produces mystic and saint.

If I am recounting it well, Jung's myth and the sense of God that pervades it is not a comfortable one. It finally leads to the question of what can be done, what attitude taken? I think the directions toward human responsibility within the wider sensitivities of Jung's myth would move along these lines: In obvious tension with orthodox claims to exclusive possessions of truth, religious or secular, we could become more aware of both the wealth and the split in the divine ground of being and of the suffering dignity bestowed upon our humanity in the divine plea to redeem its contradictions in the process of history.

In this light, premature claims to "final" systems of salvation would be more readily seen as impediments to the process of the mutual maturing of divinity and humanity in the history of human consciousness. The freeing doubt thus engendered would deprive these systems of their lethal qualities, while enabling them to contribute to the human hope for a myth with more extensive empathies than those currently ruling collective consciousness. Indeed their contribution to such hope would be all the more efficacious precisely because of their self-divestiture of claims to monopolize access to the ultimate.

But even this is too collective an approach. For, in the final analysis, Jung would seem to invite each individual to suffer some side of the divine contradiction in the depths of his or her life and to work toward its resolution as the *opus,* the work, of a lifetime. This work then becomes the truth of that life and its most precious contribution to the redemption of both humanity and divinity. In this universal priesthood, the hope of those who suffer it is supported by both sides of Jung's myth. For whoever engages in the *opus* does so with the confidence that the healing of one's own humanity is some side of the healing of God's primordial illness. This gives the work its dignity and value. But whoever engages in this work is also borne along by the confidence that the healing of the divine infirmity in one's own life is also the deepest thrust of

God's intent toward humanity and its history. This divine urgency gives the work its ultimate hope of success.

I will not violate the spirit of that saving doubt I have championed by becoming too certain of its success. To say more in the face of the mutual redemption of humanity and divinity which Jung locates at the core of the psyche and makes the centerpiece of his own myth, is to risk saying much less, and to divest the myth of its mystery. It could so easily lead to the loss of what Jung calls "the gift of doubt" and constitute a final violation of the "virginity of things beyond our ken."

I would, however, suggest that the virgin of such saving doubt yields herself only to processes more intimate, more sustained and more intense than can be publicly conveyed. For I suspect she gives herself only to those who seek her first and at length in the privacy of their souls. Finally I would urge that more would turn to seek her there. The grace of her saving doubt and her broadening empathies may now be more than a matter of rhetoric. Their cultivation may be a matter of our common survival.

Notes

CW—*The Collected Works of C.G. Jung,* 20 vols., trans. R.F.C. Hull, ed. H. Read, M. Fordham, G. Adler, Wm. McGuire, Bollingen Series XX (Princeton: Princeton University Press, 1953–1979).

1 Jung and the Coincidence of Opposites

1. See *Memories, Dreams, Reflections,* trans. Richard and Clara Winston, ed. Aniela Jaffé (New York: Vintage Books, 1961), p. 161. Here Jung states that a dream he had during a period of tension with Freud led him to posit "a collective *a priori* beneath the collective psyche."
2. See, for instance, "Psychological Commentary on *The Tibetan Book of the Dead,*" *Psychology and Religion,* CW 11, par. 845: "The archetypes are, so to speak, organs of the pre-rational psyche. They are eternally inherited forms and ideas which have at first no specific content."
3. "On the Nature of the Psyche," *The Structure and Dynamics of the Psyche,* CW 8, pars. 419f.
4. See, for instance, "Answer to Job," *Psychology and Religion,* CW 11, par. 557: "These *entia* are the archetypes of the collective unconscious, and they precipitate complexes of ideas in the form of mythological motifs."
5. See "A Psychological Approach to the Dogma of the Trinity," ibid., par. 222: "Wherever we find it, the archetype has a compelling force which it derives from the unconscious, and whenever its effect becomes conscious it has a distinctly numinous quality." See also "Psychology and Religion," ibid., par. 9, where Jung clearly relates original religious experience, and the creeds founded upon such experience, to the numinous power of the archetypes.
6. *Memories, Dreams, Reflections,* pp. 170–199.
7. See "Psychological Commentary on *The Tibetan Book of the Great Liberation,*" *Psychology and Religion,* CW 11, par. 782: "Because the unconscious is the matrix mind, the quality of creativeness attaches to it."
8. See Jung's discussion of the need to "reenter" the mother (symbolically) in *Symbols of Transformation,* CW 5, chapter 5, "Symbols of the Mother." Jung writes, "It is not incestuous cohabitation that is desired but rebirth." (par. 332)

9. See "The Undiscovered Self," *Civilization in Transition,* CW 10, par. 528. Typically Jung writes here, "If therefore the psyche is of overriding empirical importance, so also is the individual, who is the only immediate manifestation of the psyche."

10. Jung's most explicit treatment of the Self is in *Aion,* CW 9ii, chapter 4, "The Self," and chapter 14, "The Structure and Dynamics of the Self."

11. See "The Psychology of the Child Archetype," *The Archetypes and the Collective Unconscious,* CW 9i, pars. 259ff.

12. Ibid., par. 299. Here Jung relates the archetype of the child both to the "essence of man" and to the Self. He writes, "It [the child archetype] is thus both the beginning and the end, an initial and a terminal creature."

13. "Little Gidding," *Four Quartets* (London: Faber and Faber, 1944), lines 239-242.

14. Pauli's dream material is presented anonymously, and interpreted at great length, in "Individual Dream Symbolism in Relation to Alchemy," *Psychology and Alchemy,* CW 12, pars. 44ff. That the dreams are Pauli's is revealed in "The Symbolic Life," *The Symbolic Life,* CW 18, par. 673, note 9.

15. "Psychology and Religion," *Psychology and Religion,* CW 11, par. 40.

16. "Individual Dream Symbolism in Relation to Alchemy," *Psychology and Alchemy,* CW 12, pars. 164, 183.

17. "Psychology and Religion," *Psychology and Religion,* CW 11, pars. 50f, 56.

18. See, for instance, Jung's statements on this issue in "The Symbolic Life," *The Symbolic Life,* CW 18, pars. 671, 673.

19. "Psychology and Religion," *Psychology and Religion,* CW 11, par. 58.

20. For Jung's comments on the significance of "the voice" in dreams, see ibid., pars. 63ff.

21. Ibid., par. 111.

22. *Mysterium Coniunctionis,* CW 14, par. 41. Here Jung cites Bonaventure's *Itinerarium Mentis ad Deum,* chapter 5, as containing one formulation of this principle. He relates the principle to a religious description of the Self in *Psychological Types,* CW 6, par. 791, note 74, and cites it again in "A Psychological Approach to the Dogma of the Trinity," *Psychology and Religion,* CW 11, par. 229, note 6. Here he relates the principle to hermetic and gnostic traditions and to the medieval thinker, Allan de Lulle.

23. See "Transformation Symbolism in the Mass," ibid., pars. 296ff.
24. Ibid., par. 139: "The place of the deity seems to be taken by the wholeness of man."
25. Ibid., par. 105. Jung writes, "But the quaternity as produced by the modern psyche points directly not only to the God within, but to the identity of God and man."
26. Ibid. The key text reads, "The Church, it seems to me, probably has to repudiate any attempt to take such conclusions seriously. She may even have to condemn any approach to these experiences, since she cannot admit that nature unites what she herself has divided."
27. *Mysterium Coniunctionis,* CW 14, par. 760: "The creation of unity by a magical procedure meant the possibility of effecting a union with the world—not with the world of multiplicity as we see it but with a potential world, the eternal Ground of all empirical being, just as the self is the ground and origin of the individual personality past, present, and future."
28. Ibid., pars. 670, 742.
29. Ibid., par. 742: "The *unio mentalis* signified, therefore, an extension of consciousness and the governance of the soul's motions by the spirit of truth." See also ibid., par. 671.
30. On the second stage, see ibid., pars. 677, 679.
31. Ibid., par. 760.
32. Ibid., par. 761.
33. Ibid.
34. Ibid., par. 762.
35. Ibid., par. 759.
36. See "Psychology and Religion," *Psychology and Religion,* CW 11, par. 16: "As a matter of fact, the only form of existence of which we have immediate knowledge is psychic."
37. See "Concerning the Archetypes and the Anima Concept," *The Archetypes and the Collective Unconscious,* CW 9i, par. 136, and "Foreword to White's *God and the Unconscious,*" *Psychology and Religion,* CW 11, par. 454, note 3.
38. Ibid., par. 18: "Not only does the psyche exist, it is existence itself."
39. See Jung's discussion of *esse in anima,* and the creative and unitive functions of fantasy, in "The Type Problem in Classical and Mediaeval Thought," *Psychological Types,* CW 6, pars. 66f, 78, 85.
40. "On the Nature of the Psyche," *The Structure and Dynamics of the Psyche,* CW 8, par. 344.
41. Ibid.

42. See "Psychology and Religion," *Psychology and Religion,* CW 11, par. 8. Here Jung relates religion, from the original use of the word *religio,* to "a careful consideration and observation of certain dynamic factors that are conceived as 'powers,' " namely, the products of the unconscious.

43. Ibid., par. 102.

44. "A Psychological Approach to the Dogma of the Trinity," ibid., par. 170.

45. Ibid., par. 285.

46. Ibid.

47. See "Transformation Symbolism in the Mass," ibid., pars. 296ff.

48. See "Christ, A Symbol of the Self," *Aion,* CW 9ii, pars. 68ff.

49. See, for instance, "Psychology and Religion," *Psychology and Religion,* CW 11, par. 5.

2. Love, Celibacy and the Inner Marriage

1. *Memories, Dreams, Reflections,* trans. Richard and Clara Winston, ed. Aniela Jaffé (New York: Vintage Books, 1961), p. 353.

2. "The Syzygy: Anima and Animus," *Aion,* CW 9ii, par. 42.

3. *Mysterium Coniunctionis,* CW 14, par. 760.

4. *The Flowing Light of the Godhead* (The Revelations of Mechthilde of Magdeburg), trans. Lucy Menzies (London: Longmans, Green, 1953), Book 1, 44.

5. Ibid.

6. Ibid.

7. Ibid.

8. Ibid.

9. Ibid.

10. Ibid.

11. Ibid.

12. Ibid.

13. Ibid.

14. See Jung, "Answer to Job," *Psychology and Religion,* CW 11, pars. 642ff, and Edward F. Edinger, *The Creation of Consciousness: Jung's Myth for Modern Man* (Toronto: Inner City Books, 1984), pp. 59ff.

15. *The Flowing Light of the Godhead,* Book 3, 9.

16. Ibid.

17. Ibid., Book 4, 12.

18. Ibid., Book 1, 23.

19. Ibid., Book 1, 22.

20. Ibid., Book 7, 37.
21. Ibid.
22. Ibid.
23. *Symbols of Transformation*, CW 5, par. 128.
24. Ibid., par. 129.
25. Ibid., par. 130.
26. Ibid., pars. 135-138.
27. Ibid., par. 144.
28. "On the Psychology of the Unconscious," *Two Essays on Analytical Psychology*, CW 7, par. 212.
29. Ibid., par. 214.
30. Ibid., par. 215.
31. Ibid., par. 216.
32. "Transformation Symbolism in the Mass," *Psychology and Religion*, CW 11, par. 396.
33. "The Psychology of the Child Archetype," *The Archetypes and the Collective Unconscious*, CW 9i, par. 295.
34. "Gnostic Symbols of the Self," *Aion*, CW 9ii, par. 320.
35. "The Philosophical Tree," *Alchemical Studies*, CW 13, par. 389.
36. "The Type Problem in Poetry," *Psychological Types*, CW 6, par. 392.
37. Helmut Barz, *Selbst-Erfahrung: Tiefenpsychologie und christlicher Glaube* (Self-Knowledge: Depth Psychology and Christian Faith) (Stuttgart: Kreuz Verlag, 1973), pp. 140-142.

3   Jung's Understanding of Mysticism

1. *Psychological Types*, CW 6, par. 62.
2. "The Tavistock Lectures," *The Symbolic Life*, CW 18, par. 218.
3. Ibid.
4. Ibid., pars. 219f.
5. "The Philosophical Tree," *Alchemical Studies*, CW 13, par. 482.
6. *Mysterium Coniunctionis*, CW 14, par. 530.
7. "A Psychological Approach to the Dogma of the Trinity," *Psychology and Religion*, CW 11, par. 170.
8. Ibid., pars. 169ff.
9. See, for instance, "Christ, a Symbol of the Self," *Aion*, CW 9ii, pars. 68ff.
10. "Transformation Symbolism in the Mass," *Psychology and Religion*, CW 11, pars. 296ff.
11. "The Tavistock Lectures," *The Symbolic Life*, CW 18, par. 221.
12. Ibid.

13. "Transformation Symbolism in the Mass," *Psychology and Religion,* CW 11, par. 390.
14. "The Psychological Aspects of the Kore," *The Archetypes and the Collective Unconscious,* CW 9i, par. 306.
15. See *Mysterium Coniunctionis,* CW 14, par. 290, and "Transformation Symbolism in the Mass," *Psychology and Religion,* CW 11, par. 400.
16. See ibid, par. 390, where Jung describes the unconscious as "of indefinite extent with no assignable limits."
17. *Psychology and Alchemy,* CW 12, par. 11, note 6.
18. "Transformation Symbolism in the Mass," *Psychology and Religion,* CW 11, par. 396.
19. Ibid., par. 440.
20. Ibid., par. 445.
21. See *Two Essays on Analytical Psychology,* CW 7, pars. 260ff.
22. See above, chapter 1, note 22.
23. "Gnostic Symbols of the Self," *Aion,* CW 9ii, pars. 312f.
24. *Mysterium Coniunctionis,* CW 14, section 6, "The Conjunction."
25. Ibid., par. 694.
26. Ibid., par. 670.
27. Ibid., par. 773.
28. Ibid.
29. Ibid., par. 764.
30. Ibid., par. 763.
31. Ibid.
32. Ibid., par. 760.
33. Ibid., par. 718.
34. Ibid., par. 760.
35. Ibid.
36. Ibid., par. 761.
37. Ibid.
38. Ibid., par. 762.
39. Ibid., par. 662.
40. See "Synchronicity: An Acausal Connecting Principle," *The Structure and Dynamics of the Psyche,* CW 8, pars. 816ff.
41. See "Psychology and Religion," *Psychology and Religion,* CW 11, pars. 16, 18. Jung writes: "Not only does the psyche exist, it is existence itself."
42. "Psychological Commentary on *The Tibetan Book of the Great Liberation,*" ibid., par. 785.
43. "Psychological Commentary on *The Tibetan Book of the Dead,*" ibid., pars. 835f.

44. "Foreword to Suzuki's *Introduction to Zen Buddhism,*" ibid., par. 899.
45. See *C.G. Jung Letters,* ed. Gerhard Adler and Aniela Jaffé, Bollingen Series XCV (Princeton: Princeton University Press, 1975), vol. 2, p. 502, where Jung writes in a letter to J.F. Rychlak (April 27, 1959): "There is, of course, a remarkable coincidence between certain tenets of Hegelian philosophy and my findings concerning the collective unconscious."

4   Jung and Tillich Reconsidered

1. See William R. Rogers, "Tillich and Depth Psychology," *The Thought of Paul Tillich,* ed. James Luther Adams, Wilhelm Pauch, Roger L. Shinn (San Francisco: Harper and Row, 1985), p. 105. Rogers in turn is dependent on Wilhelm and Marion Pauch, *Paul Tillich: His Life and Thought* (New York: Harper and Row, 1976), vol. 1, p. 81.
2. *Mysterium Coniunctionis,* CW 14, pars. 760, 767.
3. *The Dynamics of Faith* (New York: Harper and Row, 1958), p. 53.
4. "A Psychological Approach to the Dogma of the Trinity," *Psychology and Religion,* CW 11, par. 170.
5. *Dynamics of Faith,* chapter 1, section 2, "Faith as a Centered Act," pp. 4-8.
6. Tillich, *Systematic Theology* (Chicago: University of Chicago Press, 1951), vol. 1, pp. 6-7.
7. See "The Two Types of Philosophy of Religion," in *Theology of Culture,* ed. Robert C. Kimball (Oxford: Oxford University Press, 1959), p. 18.
8. *Systematic Theology,* vol. 1, pp. 83ff, 147ff.
9. Ibid., p. 139.
10. *Pychology and Alchemy,* CW 12, par. 11, note 6.
11. *Memories, Dreams, Reflections,* ed. Aniela Jaffé (New York: Vintage Books, 1961). Jung's reflections on his father's faith are to be found on pp. 40, 42f, 46f, 52ff, 73, 75, 90ff; his remarks on pp. 93 and 215ff are especially relevant.
12. *Pychology and Alchemy,* CW 12, pars. 10, 12.
13. "Psychological Commentary on *The Tibetan Book of the Dead,*" *Psychology and Religion,* CW 11, par. 771.
14. *Systematic Theology,* vol. 1, p. 204.
15. Ibid., pp. 202f.
16. Ibid., p. 72.
17. Ibid., p. 74; see also "The Depth of Reason," pp. 79ff.
18. Ibid., pp. 251, 254ff.

19. Ibid., vol. 3, p. 421.
20. Ibid., vol. 1, pp. 250f.
21. "A Psychological Approach to the Dogma of the Trinity," *Psychology and Religion,* CW 11, section 2, "Father, Son and Spirit," pars. 194ff, and section 4, "The Three Persons in the Light of Psychology," pars. 222ff.
22. *Systematic Theology,* vol. 2, pp. 33f.
23. Ibid., p. 23.
24. Ibid., pp. 33ff.
25. Ibid., p. 36.
26. Ibid., p. 44.
27. Ibid., p. 91.
28. See *The Courage to Be* (New Haven: Yale University Press, 1952), pp. 40ff.
29. See *Systematic Theology,* vol. 1, pp. 174-186.
30. Ibid., vol. 3, part 4, 3, "The Divine Spirit and the Ambiguities of Life," pp. 162ff.
31. Ibid., pp. 406f.
32.. *The Courage to Be,* pp. 72f.
33. Ibid., p. 73.
34. Ibid., p. 74.
35. *Systematic Theology,* vol. 3, part 4, 1, A, pp. 11ff.
36. *The Courage to Be,* p. 73.
37. Ibid., p. 74.
38. *Systematic Theology,* vol. 1, "The Method of Correlation," pp. 59-66.
39. See *Memories, Dreams, Reflections,* chapter 6, "Confrontation with the Unconscious," p. 170.
40. See, for instance, "Psychology and Religion," *Psychology and Religion,* CW 11, par. 9.
41. See "Christ, A Symbol of the Self," *Aion,* CW 9ii, pars. 74, 76f.
42. "A Psychological Approach to the Dogma of the Trinity," *Psychology and Religion,* CW 11, sections 4 and 5, pars. 222ff, and conclusion, pars. 243ff.
43. Ibid.
44. See "Answer to Job," ibid., especially pars. 557ff.
45. Ibid., Prefatory Note, p. 358.
46. *Mysterium Coniunctionis,* CW 14, par. 290.
47. "The Significance of the History of Religions for the Systematic Theologian," in *The Future of Religions,* ed. Jerald C. Brauer (New York: Harper and Row, 1966), p. 91.
48. Ibid., p. 88.

49. Ibid., p. 81.
50. *Carl Gustav Jung, A Memorial Meeting* (New York: Analytical Psychology Club, 1961), p. 31.
51. Ibid., pp. 29f.

5   Jung's Impact on Theology and Religious Studies

1. See Murray Stein, *Jung's Treatment of Christianity: The Psychotherapy of a Religious Tradition* (Wilmette, Illinois: Chiron Publications, 1985), particularly chapter 1, where Stein presents an overview of Jung's interpreters to date and points to their inadequacy, and chapter 4, where he states that Jung's psychology works to transcend Christianity. See also John P. Dourley, *The Illness That We Are: A Jungian Critique of Christianity* (Toronto: Inner City Books, 1984).

2. See, for instance, "Psychology and Religion," *Psychology and Religion,* CW 11, part 1, "The Autonomy of the Unconscious," pars. 1ff.

3. See Gregory Baum, *Faith and Doctrine* (New York: Newman Press, 1969), pp. 55ff, and *Man Becoming* (New York: Herder and Herder, 1970), chapter 1, "The Blondelian Shift."

4. "Psychology and Religion," *Psychology and Religion,* CW 11, pars. 143f; "Answer to Job," ibid., pars. 755f; and "Christ, A Symbol of the Self," *Aion,* CW 9ii, par. 73.

5. "A Psychological Approach to the Dogma of the Trinity," *Psychology and Religion,* CW 11, pars. 169ff, 178, 226f, 280ff; "The Historical Significance of the Fish," *Aion,* CW 9ii, par. 170; and "The Psychology of Christian Alchemical Symbolism," ibid., pars. 270ff, 281f.

6. "Psychology and Religion," *Psychology and Religion,* CW 11, pars. 81ff; "The Alchemical Interpretation of the Fish," *Aion,* CW 9ii, pars. 260f.

7. "The Psychology of Christian Alchemical Symbolism," ibid., pars. 276ff; "Psychology and Religion," *Psychology and Religion,* CW 11, pars. 75ff.

8. Ibid., pars. 143ff; "Archetypes of the Collective Unconscious," *The Archetypes and the Collective Unconscious,* CW 9i, pars. 50ff.

9. "The Psychology of Christian Alchemical Symbolism," *Aion,* CW 9ii, pars. 272, 282.

10. "Psychology and Religion," *Psychology and Religion,* CW 11, par. 103.

11. See John P. Dourley, "Jung and Tillich Compared," *Journal of Analytical Psychology,* July 1973.

12. "A Psychological Approach to the Dogma of the Trinity," *Psychology and Religion*, CW 11, pars. 169ff.
13. Ibid., pars. 196f.
14. Ibid., par. 233.
15. Ibid., pars. 268ff.
16. "Psychology and Religion," ibid., par. 146; "A Psychological Approach to the Dogma of the Trinity," ibid., pars. 26ff; "Answer to Job," ibid., pars. 688ff.
17. "A Psychological Approach to the Dogma of the Trinity," ibid., par. 233; "Transformation Symbolism in the Mass," ibid., pars. 390ff, 410ff.
18. Ibid., pars. 414ff.
19. "Psychological Commentary on *The Tibetan Book of the Great Liberation*," ibid., pars. 762f, 773; "Psychotherapists or the Clergy," ibid., par. 522.
20. "Christ, A Symbol of the Self," *Aion*, CW 9ii, par. 73.
21. "Psychological Commentary on *The Tibetan Book of the Great Liberation*," *Psychology and Religion*, CW 11, pars. 770f; "Transformation Symbolism in the Mass," ibid., par. 447; "The Self," *Aion*, CW 9ii, par. 65.
22. "Psychology and Religion," *Psychology and Religion*, CW 11, pars. 101ff; "Psychological Commentary on *The Tibetan Book of the Dead*," ibid., par. 771; "Brother Klaus," ibid., pars. 481ff.
23. "Answer to Job," ibid., par. 741; "Foreword to Suzuki's *Introduction to Zen Buddhism*," ibid., pars. 887, 894; "Gnostic Symbols of the Self," *Aion*, CW 9ii, pars. 301ff.
24. *Memories, Dreams, Reflections*, ed. Aniela Jaffé (New York: Vintage Books, 1961), pp. 200ff.
25. "A Psychological Approach to the Dogma of the Trinity," *Psychology and Religion*, CW 11, pars. 248f; "Christ, A Symbol of the Self," *Aion*, CW 9ii, par. 112, note 74.
26. "A Psychological Approach to the Dogma of the Trinity," *Psychology and Religion*, CW 11, pars. 246ff.
27. Ibid., pars. 251f and note 13; "Foreword to Werblowsky's *Lucifer and Prometheus*," ibid., par. 469; "Answer to Job," ibid., pars. 743, 748.
28. Paul Tillich, "Two Types of Philosophy of Religion," in *Theology of Culture*, ed. R.C. Kimball (New York: Oxford Univesity Press, 1964), p. 29.
29. See "Psychology and Religion," *Psychology and Religion*, CW 11, in

which Jung describes a resolving dream as pointing to divine immanence.

30. See, for instance, "Concerning the Archetypes, with Special Reference to the Anima Concept," *The Archetypes and the Collective Unconscious,* CW 9i, par. 125; see also "Archetypes of the Collective Unconscious," ibid., par. 49, where Jung refers to the "isms" as "the present social delusional systems."

31. "Psychology and Religion," *Psychology and Religion,* CW 11, pars. 16, 18.

32. On the unity of conscious and unconscious in the birth of the Self, Jung writes: "The self then functions as a union of opposites and thus constitutes the most immediate experience of the Divine which it is psychologically possible to imagine." ("Transformation Symbolism in the Mass," ibid., par. 396) Again, referring to the power and gratuity of the unconscious in its commerce with consciousness, he writes: "The method cannot, however, produce the actual process of unconscious compensation; for that we depend upon the unconscious psyche or the 'grace of God'—names make no difference." ("Psychological Commentary on *The Tibetan Book of the Great Liberation,*" ibid., par. 779)

33. On this point Jung is explicit: "It is therefore psychologically quite unthinkable for God to be simply the 'wholly other,' for a 'wholly other' could never be one of the soul's deepest and closest intimacies, which is precisely what God is." ("Introduction to the Religious and Psychological Problems of Alchemy," *Psychology and Alchemy,* CW 12, p. 11, note 6)

34. Jung writes: "I have to ask myself also, in all seriousness, whether it might not be far more dangerous if Christian symbols were made inaccessible to thoughtful understanding by being banished to a sphere of sacrosanct unintelligibility. They can easily become so remote from us that their irrationality turns into preposterous nonsense." ("A Psychological Approach to the Dogma of the Trinity," *Psychology and Religion,* CW 11, par. 170)

35. "Answer to Job," ibid., pars. 357ff.

36. "A Psychological Approach to the Dogma of the Trinity," ibid., pars. 169ff.

37. For Jung the myth of Job captures this dialectic. "All this," he writes, "pointed to a *complexio oppositorum* and thus recalled again the story of Job to my mind: Job who expected help from God against God." (Prefatory Note to "Answer to Job," ibid., p. 358)

38. This is implied throughout Jung's thought and explicit in this passage: "The conscious mind does not embrace the totality of man, for this totality consists only partly of his conscious contents, and for the other and far greater part, of his unconscious, which is of indefinite extent with no assignable limits." ("Transformation Symbolism in the Mass," ibid., par. 390)

39. Arguing that the unconscious extends to the human condition itself the unity of divine and human natures—the *homoousia* that in orthodox dogma is attributed only to Christ—Jung writes: "The Church, it seems to me, probably has to repudiate any attempt to take such conclusions seriously . . . since she cannot admit that nature unites what she herself has divided." ("Psychology and Religion," ibid., par. 105) Jung adds: "That is to say, what happens in the life of Christ happens always and everywhere." (Ibid., par. 106)

40. This is particularly evident throughout his "Transformation Symbolism in the Mass," ibid.

41. See "Christ, A Symbol of the Self," *Aion,* CW 9ii, par. 69.

42. Ibid., pars. 122f.

43. The role of compensation in the production of religion by the unconscious is a subject that deserves more study. Let it simply be noted here that Jung believes religions arise out of the unconscious in order to compensate collective one-sidedness, and so always in relation or response to a particular social order (or disorder). This social dimension does not mitigate the locating of the genesis of religion in the unconscious; rather for Jung the social dimension serves only to determine what form religion will take in its social-historical concretion.

6 Of Human Faiths and Kidney Stones

1. "Psychology and Religion," *Psychology and Religion,* CW 11, par. 86.

2. Ibid., par. 23.

3. Ibid.

4. *C.G. Jung Letters,* ed. Gerhard Adler and Aniela Jaffé, Bollingen Series XCV (Princeton: Princeton University Press, 1973), vol. 2, p. 138.

5. Ibid.

6. See "Answer to Job," *Psychology and Religion,* CW 11, pars. 564ff, 747. See also the authoritative discussion by Edward F. Edinger in *The Creation of Consciousness: Jung's Myth for Modern Man*

(Toronto: Inner City Books, 1984), chapter 3, "Depth Psychology as the New Dispensation: Reflections on Jung's 'Answer to Job.'"

7. Ibid., par. 747.
8. Ibid., par. 647.
9. Ibid., par. 740.
10. See "A Psychological Approach to the Dogma of the Trinity," ibid., par. 259.
11. "Answer to Job," ibid., par. 728.
12. *Psychology and Alchemy,* CW 12, par. 8.
13. See, for instance, "Archetypes of the Collective Unconscious," *Archetypes and the Collective Unconscious,* CW 9i, par. 125.

Index

CATALOGUE

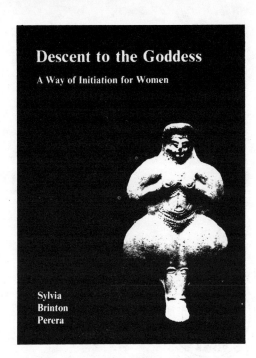

Descent to the Goddess

A Way of Initiation for Women

Sylvia
Brinton
Perera

6. Descent to the Goddess: A Way of Initiation for Women. $10
Sylvia Brinton Perera (New York). ISBN 0-919123-05-8. 112 pages.

This is a highly original and provocative book about women's freedom and the need for an inner, female authority in a masculine-oriented society.

Combining ancient texts and modern dreams, the author, a practising therapist, presents a way of feminine initiation. Inanna-Ishtar, Sumerian Goddess of Heaven and Earth, journeys into the underworld to Ereshkigal, her dark "sister," and returns. So modern women must descend from their old role-determined behavior into the depths of their instinct and image patterns, to find anew the Great Goddess and restore her values to modern culture.

Men too will be interested in this book, both for its revelations of women's essential nature and for its implications in terms of their own inner journey.

"The most significant contribution to an understanding of feminine psychology since Esther Harding's *Way of All Women*."—**Marion Woodman,** psychoanalyst and author of *The Owl Was a Baker's Daughter.*

Addiction to Perfection
The Still Unravished Bride

A Psychological Study by
Marion Woodman

12. Addiction to Perfection: The Still Unravished Bride.
Marion Woodman (Toronto). ISBN 0-919123-11-2. 208 pages. $12

"This book is about taking the head off an evil witch." With these words Marion Woodman begins her spiral journey, a powerful and authoritative look at the psychology and attitudes of modern woman.

The witch is a Medusa or a Lady Macbeth, an archetypal pattern functioning autonomously in women, petrifying their spirit and inhibiting their development as free and creatively receptive individuals. Much of this, according to the author, is due to a cultural one-sidedness that favors patriarchal values—productivity, goal orientation, intellectual excellence, spiritual perfection, etc.—at the expense of more earthy, interpersonal values that have traditionally been recognized as the heart of the feminine.

Marion Woodman's first book, *The Owl Was a Baker's Daughter: Obesity, Anorexia Nervosa and the Repressed Feminine,* focused on the psychology of eating disorders and weight disturbances.

Here, with a broader perspective on the same general themes, Marion Woodman continues her remarkable exploration of women's mysteries through case material, dreams, literature and mythology, in food rituals, rape symbolism, Christianity, imagery in the body, sexuality, creativity and relationships.

The final chapter, a discussion of the psychological meaning of ravishment (as opposed to rape), celebrates the integration of body and spirit and shows what this can mean to a woman in terms of her personal independence.

Studies in Jungian Psychology
by Jungian Analysts

LIMITED EDITION PAPERBACKS

Prices quoted are in U.S. dollars (except for Canadian orders)

1. **The Secret Raven: Conflict and Transformation.**
Daryl Sharp (Toronto). ISBN 0-919123-00-7. 128 pp. $10
A practical study of *puer aeternus* psychology, with special attention to dream interpretation, the provisional life, relationships, mid-life crisis, the mother complex and Jung's concepts of anima and shadow. Illustrated.

2. **The Psychological Meaning of Redemption Motifs in Fairytales.**
Marie-Louise von Franz (Zurich). ISBN 0-919123-01-5. 128 pp. $10
A unique account of the significance of fairytales for an understanding of individuation. Particularly helpful for its symbolic approach to the meaning of typical dream motifs (bathing, beating, clothes, animals, etc.).

3. **On Divination and Synchronicity:**
The Psychology of Meaningful Chance.
Marie-Louise von Franz (Zurich). ISBN 0-919123-02-3. 128 pp. $10
A penetrating study of the meaning of time, number and methods of divining fate such as the I Ching and astrology, contrasting Western scientific ideas with those of the Chinese and so-called primitives. Illustrated.

4. **The Owl Was a Baker's Daughter:**
Obesity, Anorexia Nervosa and the Repressed Feminine.
Marion Woodman (Toronto). ISBN 0-919123-03-1. 144 pp. $10
A modern classic in feminine psychology, with particular attention to the body as mirror of the psyche in eating disorders and weight disturbances. Explores the personal and cultural loss of the feminine principle, through case studies, dreams, Christianity and mythology. Illustrated.

5. **Alchemy: Introduction to the Symbolism and the Psychology.**
Marie-Louise von Franz (Zurich). ISBN 0-919123-04-X. 288 pp. $16
A detailed guide to what the alchemists were really looking for: emotional balance and wholeness. Invaluable for interpreting images and motifs in modern dreams. Completely demystifies the subject. **84 Illustrations.**

6. **Descent to the Goddess. A Way of Initiation for Women.**
Sylvia Brinton Perera (New York). ISBN 0-919123-05-8. 112 pp. $10
A timely and provocative study of the need for an inner, female authority in a masculine-oriented society. Based on the Sumerian goddess Inanna-Ishtar's journey to the underworld, her transformation and her return. Rich in insights from dreams, mythology and analysis. (See also title 23)

7. **The Psyche as Sacrament: C.G. Jung and Paul Tillich.**
John P. Dourley (Ottawa). ISBN 0-919123-06-6. 128 pp. $10
A comparative study from a dual perspective (author is Catholic priest and Jungian analyst), examining the psychological meaning of God, Christ, the Trinity, the Spirit, morality and religion. (See also title 17.)